PERFORMATIVITY

Do our writings and our utterances reflect or describe the world, or do they intervene in it? Do they, perhaps, help to make it? If so, how? Within what limits and with what implications? Contemporary theorists have considered the ways in which the languages we speak might be 'performative' in just this way, and their thinking on the topic has had important impact on a broad range of academic disciplines.

In this accessible introduction to a sometimes complex field, James Loxley:

- offers a concise and original account of critical debates around the idea of performativity
- traces the history of the concept through the work of such influential theorists as J. L. Austin, John Searle, Stanley Fish, Jacques Derrida, Paul de Man and Judith Butler
- examines the implications of performativity for fields such as literary and cultural theory, philosophy, performance studies, and the theory of gender and sexuality
- emphasises political and ethical implications that its most important theorists have drawn from the notion of performativity
- suggests ways in which major debates around the topic have obscured its alternative interpretations and uses.

For students trying to make sense of performativity and related concepts such as the speech act, 'ordinary language', and iterability, and for those seeking to understand the place of these ideas in contemporary performance theory, this clear guide will prove indispensable. *Performativity* offers not only a path through challenging critical terrain, but a new understanding of just what is at stake in the exploration of this field.

James Loxley is Senior Lecturer in English Literature at the University of Edinburgh. He is the author of several books and articles on seventeenth century literature and on literary theory and philosophy.

THE NEW CRITICAL IDIOM

SERIES EDITOR: JOHN DRAKAKIS, UNIVERSITY OF STIRLING

The New Critical Idiom is an invaluable series of introductory guides to today's critical terminology. Each book:

- provides a handy, explanatory guide to the use (and abuse) of the term
- offers an original and distinctive overview by a leading literary and cultural critic
- relates the term to the larger field of cultural representation

With a strong emphasis on clarity, lively debate and the widest possible breadth of examples, *The New Critical Idiom* is an indispensable approach to key topics in literary studies.

Also available in this series:

PERFORMATIVITY

James Loxley

Routledge
Taylor & Francis Group

LONDON AND NEW YORK

First published 2007
by Routledge
2 Park Square, Milton Park, Abingdon, Oxon OX14 4RN

Simultaneously published in the USA and Canada
by Routledge
270 Madison Ave, New York, NY 10016

Routledge is an imprint of the Taylor & Francis Group, *an informa business*

© 2007 James Loxley

Typeset in Garamond and Scala Sans by Taylor & Francis Books

Printed and bound in Great Britain by
TJI Digital, Padstow, Cornwall

British Library Cataloguing in Publication Data
A catalogue record for this book is available from the British Library
Library of Congress Cataloging in Publication Data
Loxley, James, 1968-
  Performativity / James Loxley.
      p. cm. -- (The new critical idiom)
  Includes bibliographical references and index.
1. Speech acts (Linguistics) 2. Performative (Philosophy) I. Title.
  P95.55.L69 2006
  401'.41--dc22

                            2006031947

ISBN10: 0-415-32925-6   ISBN13: 978-0-415-32925-5 (hbk)
ISBN10: 0-415-32926-4   ISBN13: 978-0-415-32926-2 (pbk)
ISBN10: 0-203-39128-4   ISBN13: 978-0-203-39128-0 (ebk)

CONTENTS

SERIES EDITOR'S PREFACE

The New Critical Idiom is a series of introductory books which seeks to extend the lexicon of literary terms, in order to address the radical changes which have taken place in the study of literature during the last decades of the twentieth century. The aim is to provide clear, well-illustrated accounts of the full range of terminology currently in use, and to evolve histories of its changing usage.

The current state of the discipline of literary studies is one where there is considerable debate concerning basic questions of terminology. This involves, among other things, the boundaries which distinguish the literary from the non-literary; the position of literature within the larger sphere of culture; the relationship between literatures of different cultures; and questions concerning the relation of literary to other cultural forms within the context of interdisciplinary studies.

It is clear that the field of literary criticism and theory is a dynamic and heterogeneous one. The present need is for individual volumes on terms which combine clarity of exposition with an adventurousness of perspective and a breadth of application. Each volume will contain as part of its apparatus some indication of the direction in which the definition of particular terms is likely to move, as well as expanding the disciplinary boundaries within which some of these terms have been traditionally contained. This will involve some re-situation of terms within the larger field of cultural representation, and will introduce examples from the area of film and the modern media in addition to examples from a variety of literary texts.

ACKNOWLEDGEMENTS

I am very grateful to all those with whom I have discussed the ideas presented in this book over the years, and especially to Mark Robson for the benefit of more than a few conversations around the topic. Liz Thompson and John Drakakis provided invaluable advice at the outset and conclusion of this project. I would like also to acknowledge a debt to Stanley Cavell, who kindly allowed me to look over some of his recent writing on Austin in advance of its publication, while my colleagues and the department of English Literature at Edinburgh have once again provided a supportive environment in which to work. Particular and heartfelt thanks are due to my dearest friend and wife, Joanna, without whose love and support I would never have written a word. Thanks, finally, to our children, Adam and Anna, who have demonstrated that a buggy in the porch is the surest sign, in fact the vehicle, of promise. This one is for them.

INTRODUCTION

This book tells the story of a concept. It traces the history of the 'performative' and the 'performativity' that it is held to embody from its first formulation by the English philosopher J. L. Austin in the 1950s through to its significance for contemporary theories of culture, language, identity and performance. This history arguably extends far back behind its supposed inventor (see Smith 1990 and Nerlich and Clarke 1996), but since Austin it has been both meandering and chequered. The concept of performativity has been invoked often in perfunctory or incompatible ways in recent decades; as a concept apparently proper to a trend in the philosophy of language known as 'speech act theory' it has also been the focus for one of the most notorious spats of recent critical times, when the American philosopher John Searle and his French counterpart Jacques Derrida took aim at each other over the latter's reading of Austin's work. With the assistance of an enthusiastic supporting cast the row was kept alive for nearly two decades; it ensured that the arcane details of speech act theory became one of the testing grounds in the 1980s for academic disputes surrounding 'literary theory', and for the competing claims of the Anglo-American and 'continental' approaches to philosophy. Yet Austin's legacy was an important presence in the philosophical and literary critical debate over the nature and status of language before Searle first tried to read Derrida, and his ideas on performativity were already well established as an almost irresistible springboard for thinkers and theorists keen to launch their own interventions into ongoing debates.

This is perhaps because there is something both immediately convincing and yet still striking about Austin's basic position. Austin points up the way in which our utterances can be *performative*: words do something in the world, something that is not just a matter of generating consequences, like persuading or amusing or alarming an audience. The promises, assertions, bets, threats and thanks that we offer one another are not this kind of action; but nor are they the linguistic description of non-linguistic actions going on elsewhere: they are actions *in themselves*, actions of a distinctively linguistic kind. They are 'performed', like other actions, or take place, like other worldly events, and thus make a difference in the world; it could be said that they produce a different world, even if only for a single speaker and a single addressee. As one writer on performance theory puts it, citing her own attempt at a swift explanation for a slightly sceptical audience, Austin 'argued that words are not purely reflective . . . that linguistic acts don't simply reflect a world but that speech actually has the power to *make* a world' (Jackson 2004: 2). It is the challenge this presents to accounts of language as principally descriptive in its functions that most concerns philosophers. The creative connotations of this 'making' have also drawn in theorists of literary language, and a possible relation to theatrical performance has stimulated the interest of thinkers on drama. Under these conditions performativity has become, in the acute words of one of my colleagues, a 'carry-home concept': it appears to focus a valuable but not too difficult idea, detachable from the circumstances of its formulation without significant loss and usefully applicable to a wide range of differing intellectual challenges or problems.

For these reasons, then, telling its story has long involved more than outlining its exposition by Austin. There is even a standard narrative of its origins and subsequent travels often encountered in literary or cultural theory, which usually runs as follows. Austin broadened his basic outline of the performative into a theory of 'speech acts', in which the performativity of requests, orders, declarations and so on was seen to characterise all the utterances we issue as speakers; as a key part of his argument, he portrayed fictional or literary utterances as fundamentally derivative, 'parasitic' on the serious or substantial speech acts he was theorising. John Searle then took up and elaborated this outline, producing a more general 'speech act theory' that fulfilled what Austin had only been able to sketch out, preserving and elaborating his account of fictional or 'non-serious' utterances. More radical thinkers such as Stanley Fish, Shoshana Felman and Jacques Derrida then took hold of speech act theory and decisively undid or deconstructed the attempt to demarcate a precise boundary between 'real' and 'fictional' utterances, with profound consequences for the project as a whole. Feminist and queer theorists such as Judith Butler and Eve Kosofsky Sedgwick absorbed the deconstructive lesson and applied this retooled concept of performativity to dominant or common sense claims about the identity categories of sex, gender and sexuality, thus applying the theoretical insights of deconstruction to pressing issues in cultural politics. Such illumination of the ways in which we 'act' our identities also had radical implications for how we might think about the relation between theatrical performance and the apparently real or serious world offstage, implications that performance theorists have themselves sought to spell out in recent years.

The standard narrative has its purposes. It can contextualise the concept of the performative for those who are relatively new to the topic; its sense of who the most significant figures in this story are is not at all contentious. Consequently, the reader will find all of its various moments in the chapters that follow, and a structure to the book that mirrors the customary trajectory. But grounds for concern arise as soon as the opening moves of this standard narrative are examined more closely. An account of the philosophical context of Austin's conception of the speech act is rarely offered, and thus the basis for his interest in how words might do things in and to the world often goes unexplored. The assumption appears to be that no such exploration is necessary or relevant; and indeed, one can perfectly well offer a basic outline of an apparently self-contained, easily portable 'speech act theory' without it. But the Austin who emerges from such accounts is often a rather strange figure, and one who provokes some strange reactions. He is a writer in 'a common-sense style typical of Anglo-American philosophy . . .

at its most infuriating' (Reinelt 2002: 203), or the blinkered peddler of an 'anti-theatrical performativity' that can be added 'to the long list of anti-theatrical prejudices that have vexed Western intellectual history' (Jackson 2004: 3). Worse, much worse, the American critic J. Hillis Miller has argued that Austin's account of the speech act 'reinforces a certain vision of history' that has 'the white male English philosopher, not surprisingly, as its evolutionary goal' (Miller 2001: 58). Austin is apparently keen to ensure an 'authoritarian, patriarchal imposition of law and order' (Miller 2001: 56). His philosophy, which Miller claims is contemptuous of 'ordinary language', and by implication of the 'ordinary people' who speak it, is thus an attempt to secure for himself the power and right to make all the important decisions. 'This', Miller claims, 'explains the urgency and determination with which Austin seeks to establish a sound doctrine of performative utterances. The stability of civil society and the security of the nation depends [sic] on it' (Miller 2001: 57). One could almost imagine the author of such an authoritarian doctrine supporting or collaborating with a fascist government, perhaps even writing for one of its newspapers. It is clearly doubtful that such thought could really have much to contribute to the sophisticated work of contemporary theory, and thus it is that Austin is not infrequently wheeled on only to serve as a foil for apparently more nuanced, less prejudicial approaches to the topic.

Such reactions, I want to suggest, are wrong-headed – hopelessly so, in Miller's case. Many of Austin's other critics, including Derrida, Felman and Sedgwick, have paid tribute to the playfulness, complexity and radical promise of his writing. Felman has even described it as seductive (Felman 2002: 48). They testify, though, to a recognition that Austin's account of performativity has broader implications, particularly of an ethical or political kind. Why such implications should be so badly misconstrued, or construed in so rigid and limited a fashion, is a question worth asking; the answer lies, I think, in the way in which the exchange between Searle and Derrida framed the reception of Austin's work in literary and cultural theory. In conducting their dispute, neither party was able to acknowledge that his own account of Austin might not encapsulate the body of work that had provided the occasion for confrontation. As the American philosopher Stanley Cavell puts it, neither 'really felt that Austin's is a (philosophical) voice whose signature it is *difficult* to assess and important to hear out in its difference' (Cavell 1994: 61). It is the assumption that Austin's work presents no real challenge to its readers, that its philosophical or theoretical status is swiftly registered, that has engendered the confidence with which that work is then summed up and criticised in many accounts of performativity.

In the pages that follow, I do not proceed with this kind of confidence. Following Cavell, I try to register what has often been forgotten or overlooked about Austin's philosophical 'voice' in introducing his work. My narrative both tracks and disrupts the standard model, rereading the subsequent history of performativity in the light of this more thoroughgoing engagement with its origins. The book thus begins with two chapters that offer a detailed exposition both of Austin's thinking on the speech act and its place in his broader practice as a philosopher of 'ordinary language'. It then explores the way in which Austin's ideas were taken up and rendered systematic in the work of John Searle, an appropriation which was in fact as much the transformation as the perfection of the Austinian project. My fourth chapter examines Searle's attempt to broaden his speech act approach in order to formulate a theory of fiction on the basis of scattered remarks left by Austin, and the responses to such a characterisation by Stanley Fish and Jacques Derrida. Chapter five explores the further ramifications of the deconstructive unsettling of 'speech act theory', unpacking in particular the implications of the latter's focus on the 'iterability' or repeatability of the speech act. In chapter six, the take-up of both Derrida and Austin by Judith Butler is examined and assessed, and the innovations and revisions that characterise her appropriation of performativity are set out. The final chapter returns to the question of the 'non-serious' speech act as it intersects with contemporary performance theory, and explores the relations between the often criticised Austinian lineage and the attempts by theorists of performance to put the distinction between stage and world under pressure. In all of this, I try not only to set out the various thinkers' positions and their implications, but also to attend to the different histories of performativity that are implicit in their elaboration of their own ideas. Attending to this difference requires us to refrain from assuming that the interpretations of earlier work by those coming after it are necessarily complete, correct, or final. In this way, the book seeks both to tell the story of the concept of performativity for those who have not yet heard it all before, and to suggest to those who have that there may still be more to hear.

1

FROM THE PERFORMATIVE TO THE SPEECH ACT

J. L. AUSTIN

> You are more than entitled not to know what the word 'performative'
> means. It is a new word and an ugly word, and perhaps it does not
> mean anything very much. But at any rate there is one thing in its
> favour, it is not a profound word.
>
> (Austin 1979: 233)

In 1955, John Langshaw Austin delivered the William James Lectures
at Harvard University. In the series Austin refined ideas he had begun
to explore in both a course on 'Words and Deeds' at Oxford and a couple
of the relatively few articles he had by then published, work which had
already won him a more than parochial fame. The series of twelve lectures was not, however, all that warmly received: an audience of hun-
dreds for the first had dwindled to 'a core of some twelve to fifteen
souls' by the last, 'and not all of these few were happy' (Cavell 1984:
30). A junior fellow of the University named Paul de Man heard only
that 'a somewhat odd and quirky Oxford don was giving a series of
rather dull and fairly inscrutable lectures' (Miller 2001: 61). Needless to

say, he did not feel moved to attend. After Austin's early death in 1960 the notes from which his Harvard lectures were delivered were prepared for publication and appeared in book form as *How To Do Things With Words* in 1962. Once they were in the hands of a wider audience, the indifference with which they had apparently first been greeted was replaced by an interest that has not only been sustained over decades, but has also repeatedly managed to renew itself just when it seemed at last to be exhausted. Such success has not been without its consequences: proving so open to a variety of appropriations, Austin's thinking has sometimes disappeared into the accounts of his work preferred by his inheritors. It is therefore as well for anyone concerned to map any of the more oblique peregrinations of the performative to begin by tracking some of his formulations as closely as possible.

CONSTATIVES AND PERFORMATIVES

At the outset of his first lecture, Austin draws a defining contrast between two views of language. On one side, there is the view he attributes to the 'logical positivism' that was such a force in Anglophone philosophy during the first half or so of the twentieth century: that the normal or defining business of language is making statements, such as 'it is raining' or 'the cat is on the mat', and that such statements are to be assessed in terms of their truth (their correspondence to the given facts of a situation) or their falsity (the failure of any such correspondence). Grammarians and philosophers have certainly not failed to notice that language can be used in other ways, for asking questions, or exclaiming, or issuing commands, but these uses have tended to be treated as peculiar departures from the customary linguistic business of reporting reality. This view of language is termed 'the descriptive fallacy': the mistaken assumption that language use is essentially *constative*, aimed at the production of true or false statements or descriptions.

Against this emphasis on the centrality of the constative, Austin sets the claims of those sentences fallaciously presented as special uses or departures from a descriptive norm. These are sentences that share the grammatical form of statements, and might perhaps be assumed to be such, were it not for some apparently distinctive features. Firstly, 'they do not "describe" or "report" or constate anything at all, are not "true or false"'; and secondly, 'the uttering of the sentence is, or is a part of, the doing of an action, which again would not *normally* be described as, or as "just", saying something' (Austin 1975: 5). The examples he then cites make clear the kind of utterance he has in mind: 'I do', spoken as part of the marriage service; 'I name this ship the *Queen Elizabeth*', spoken when breaking a bottle against the hull of the ship in question; 'I give and bequeath my watch to my brother', occurring in a will; 'I bet you sixpence it will rain tomorrow'. Austin comments:

> In these examples it seems clear that to utter the sentence (in, of course, the appropriate circumstances) is not to *describe* my doing of what I should be said in so uttering to be doing or to state that I am doing it: it is to do it.
>
> (Austin 1975: 6)

To say, in these instances, is to do: for this reason, Austin christens this kind of sentence or utterance *performative*, to make clear that here 'the issuing of the utterance is the performing of an action' (Austin 1975: 6).

This fundamental separation of the performative from the constative issues immediately in some significant consequences, which Austin then goes on to spell out. For a start, the criterion of validity or justification to which constative utterances are liable, that of truth considered as the correspondence of a statement to the facts of a particular situation, can't be said to apply in quite the same way to performatives, because the utterance is already a part, and perhaps the most important part, of the facts: there is no separation, and therefore no relation for us to assess, between utterance and situation. The utterance is not setting out to *describe* a situation, an event or an action: it *is* an event or an action. Saying 'the cat is on the mat' is valid in being true; to see if it is true, we need only take a quick look at the relative positions of cat and mat. To attempt to do the same with 'I bet you sixpence it will rain tomorrow' would be absurd. In this case the criterion of correspondence to the facts could not apply, unless we wanted to claim that the words spoken were merely the outward report or description of some inward spiritual or mental act. Austin is aware that this is just the view taken by those in the grip of an essentially constative model of language, and that such a view has a long lineage: he cites the title character of Euripides's play, *Hippolytus*, as giving voice to the notion that the tongue might swear to do something, but this wouldn't matter if the heart hadn't underpinned this oath with one of its own (Austin 1975: 9–10). Against this view he sets the fact that performative utterances just don't function in this manner. If I say 'I bet' or 'I do' in the appropriate circumstances I have made a bet or married, regardless of any mental reservations I was having at the time; if I say 'I promise', you would expect to hold me to it, even if I think I didn't really mean it when I said it. 'Accuracy and morality alike', Austin declares, 'are on the side of the plain saying that *our word is our bond*' (Austin 1975: 10).

INFELICITIES

There is, though, more to a performative than this. Even if it cannot be simply true or false, its validity can still be assessed: we have only to consider the matter of the 'appropriate circumstances' mentioned by Austin in order to show how. Not every utterance of the words 'I do', for example, produces a marriage, and nor does saying 'I name this ship the *Queen Elizabeth*' in front of a suitable vessel necessarily result in a ship being so named. Performatives are dependent for their validity on circumstances in precisely the way that a marriage can only be said to have taken place if the right words were said at the right time in the right place, if the right kind of person was officiating, if the contracting parties were not somehow ineligible on grounds of age or species, or already married to someone else. There are, then, lots of different ways in which a performative utterance might go wrong and fail to take effect, or else do so only problematically. A consideration of these various possible difficulties serves to show what the conditions for a successful performative must be, and in his second lecture Austin is able to tabulate six rules that encompass these conditions. They are quoted here in full.

(A.1) There must exist an accepted conventional procedure having a certain conventional effect, that procedure to include the uttering of certain words by certain persons in certain circumstances, and further,

(A.2) the particular persons and circumstances in a given case must be appropriate for the invocation of the particular procedure invoked.

(B.1) The procedure must be executed by all participants both correctly and

(B.2) completely.

(γ. 1) Where, as often, the procedure is designed for use by persons having certain thoughts or feelings, or for the inauguration of certain consequential conduct on the part of the participant, then a person participating in and so invoking the procedure must in fact have those thoughts or feelings, and the participants must intend so to conduct themselves, and further

(γ.2) must actually so conduct themselves subsequently.

(Austin 1975: 15)

The picture of the performative that emerges from this account of its enabling conditions is necessarily complex, much more so than the baldly unilinear definition of constatives with which Austin began. Statements could be valid in being true or invalid in being false, and that was seemingly all there was to say on the matter; with performative utterances, on the other hand, there were a number of different axes along which validity could be assessed. If all these conditions were met, a performative could be said to be successful or − in Austin's preferred terminology − 'felicitous' or 'happy'.

What, though, if only some of them were met? What would we say of the improvised wedding, sincerely meant but following no conventional procedure? Could that be said to have inaugurated a marriage? And what if the cleric or registrar conducting proceedings had been defrocked or improperly appointed? What if one party made a mix up of the other's name? Would it make a difference if part of the ceremony was omitted by mistake, or if a bomb scare caused its abandonment before its completion? A bigamous marriage would be infelicitous if marriage required monogamy, but would one entered into by someone under duress or the influence of alcohol be problematic in quite the same way? Austin divides the various kinds of ill that might afflict an attempted performative utterance into two major classes, and it is crucial to an understanding of tensions that emerge at the heart of his thinking to acknowledge this division. First there are the violations of the four rules A.1 to B.2, which are violations of the conventional procedures necessary for the successful accomplishment of the performance. Attempted performances thus afflicted are called *misfires*: in such circumstances 'the act in question, e.g. marrying, is not successfully performed at all, does not come off, is not achieved' (Austin 1975: 16). These were to be categorically distinguished from violations of rules γ.1

and γ.2 (hence the use of the Greek letter gamma to mark these off from the Roman A and B), which Austin terms *abuses*. In these cases, where there is something like a fundamental failure of intention or accomplishment, the infelicity does not result in a 'void' or 'empty' performance, one which simply failed to take place: instead, the act *is* accomplished, and is 'hollow' rather than empty (Austin 1975: 16). Thus we can still be bound by a promise we didn't mean, or married if we plight our troth when drunk. The gap between an 'inward' state of mind and an 'outward' verbal performance, so comprehensively dismissed when it seemed to allow the model of constative language to characterise all utterance, is here readmitted to the picture. It is a subtly different gap now: Austin had been objecting to an attempt to define performative utterances as merely constative reports of inward, silent actions or performances, not states of mind, and if no such attempt is taking place he is quite happy to admit a difference between intention and performance. It is a difference that will come to matter to many of his readers.

Misfires and abuses are further subdivided in subsequent passages in such a way as to furnish the violation of each of Austin's six rules with its own name. Thus rule A.1 is transgressed by the misinvocation of a procedure, or by an attempt to invoke a procedure where one has never been or is no longer accepted. It is unlikely, for instance, that I would respond to someone who challenged me to a duel by agreeing to settle our differences on the field of honour at dawn the next day. Where rule A.2 is violated, a misapplication has occurred: a horse has been appointed consul, or a married person has attempted to marry again, or a 'low type' has sauntered up to a vessel and crashed a bottle of champagne against it before proclaiming, 'I name this ship the *Mr Stalin*', when the ship wasn't to be so named, or at least not by him. The transgression of rule B.1 is identified as the introduction of a flaw into the execution of the procedure; that of rule B.2 as a hitch that results in its premature termination.

The abuses that violate the γ-rules call for a slightly different characterisation: problems arise as a result of participants not having the right feelings, thoughts or intentions to make the performance thoroughly felicitous, though it should be reiterated that performances thus affected are not thereby rendered void. Interestingly, Austin is in the end as concerned with the closely related class of *mistakes* as he is with these kinds of abuses. What do we say about a guilty verdict pronounced upon someone who did not, in fact, commit the crime? What, more trivially, of a penalty awarded in a football match when no foul had, in fact, been committed? In these circumstances the performative is certainly not void: the 'criminal' will be punished, the penalty may be converted and the result of the game decided. The judge, jury and referee were certainly the duly appointed and therefore appropriate people to render these verdicts, but that they are such does not exempt the utterance from accusations of invalidity: specifically, the claim that they were wrong. While this is not the same as the claim that their utterances were *false statements*, it is nonetheless returning such utterances to a territory more clearly proximate to the constative. The very precise classificatory distinction of performative and constative seems to be coming under some pressure.

Before pondering the significance of this, though, it is important to note Austin's concern with specifying the broader reach of his various kinds of infelicity. Most of them turn out not to have their source in the structure of the performative utterance as such, but apply in general to these utterances because performatives make use of characteristics or elements that are not theirs alone. Firstly, performative utterances are exposed to trouble because they are *conventional* – ritual, ceremonial – performances. Not all ritual need involve the utterance of words; but to the extent that such utterances invoke a conventional procedure, then they are in danger of suffering from the kinds of misfire or abuse to which conventional procedures are vulnerable. Secondly, insofar as performatives are *actions*, they are 'subject to certain whole dimensions of unsatisfactoriness' that afflict actions in general, both verbal and otherwise:

> I mean that actions in general (not all) are liable, for example, to be done under duress, or by accident, or owing to this or that variety of mistake, say, or otherwise unintentionally. In many such cases we are certainly unwilling to say of some such act simply that it was done or that he did it. . . . Features of this sort would normally come under the heading of 'extenuating circumstances' or of 'factors reducing or abrogating the agent's responsibility'.
>
> (Austin 1975: 21)

When he gave this lecture at Harvard Austin had already made an investigation of precisely this general liability of actions, in a paper later published under the title 'A Plea for Excuses'. Alongside his lecture series he was also teaching a graduate seminar on excuses at Harvard, which must have covered the same ground, so it is perhaps understandable that he merely notes the question at this point, alluding to it again in his treatment of mistaken performatives in remarking that 'mistake will not in general make an act *void*, though it may make it *excusable*' (Austin 1975: 42). At his death he left an unfinished piece, 'Three Ways of Spilling Ink', revisiting the topic. This investigation of the kinds of consideration that might count as an excuse for a performed action was a means to establishing an account of what action, at its most general, might be.

THE QUESTION OF THE 'NON-SERIOUS' PERFORMATIVE

So some of the kinds of infelicity from which performatives can suffer are to be explained by their belonging to the larger classes of conventional entities, on the one hand, and modes of action on the other. There is, though, a third general vulnerability to be invoked:

> As *utterances*, our performatives are *also* heir to certain other kinds of ill which infect *all* utterances . . . I mean, for example, the following: a performative utterance will, for example, be *in a peculiar way* hollow or void if said by an actor on the stage, or if introduced in a poem, or spoken in soliloquy. This applies in a similar manner to any and every utterance – a sea-change in special circumstances. Language in such circumstances is in special ways – intelligibly – used not seriously, but in ways *parasitic* upon its normal use – ways which fall under the doctrine of the *etiolations* of language.
>
> (Austin 1975: 21–22)

It is important to get the measure of this passage, since it has been the focus of much subsequent attention. Utterances – '*all* utterances', utterances *as such* – can be quoted, cited, or repeated beyond their normal conditions of employment. This is, therefore, a mundane or ordinary business: it goes on all the time, all over the place. Austin will reiterate the point further on in the lecture series by describing language, insofar as it is a kind of grammatical structure, as '*essentially* mimicable, reproducible' (Austin 1975: 96; my emphasis). So reproducibility is an essential feature of language, a possibility necessarily inhering in the linguistic materials of utterance. To speak of language in this way is to characterise it as primarily conventional: this kind of vulnerability is therefore aligned with that which is rather sketchily declared to affect conventional procedures in general. It is also to ensure that the workings of language are themselves involved in the account of how performatives do, or fail to do, their work. He addresses this concern with mimicry at greater length in a later paper, 'Pretending', and thus stitches a discussion of these issues back into the exploration of action recounted in 'A Plea for Excuses' and 'Three Ways of Spilling Ink'.

Despite both their scope and their relevance to the matter at hand, Austin takes these claims regarding actions, conventions, and utterances in general no further. Indeed, he curtails his consideration of non-serious performatives with the emphatic declaration, 'all this we are *excluding* from consideration', just as he has earlier said of the ills besetting actions in general, 'we are not including this kind of unhappiness' (Austin 1975: 21–22). It is hard to see how such acts of exclusion can be anything other than provisional given what he has said about the ubiquity and centrality of these kinds of infelicity, and his attention to them elsewhere, but his remarks have nonetheless been taken by some readers to indicate a more fundamental and telling exclusion of the fictional. Thus, for example, J. Hillis Miller calls 'the distinction between felicitous and "literary"' performatives (if that is even the best way of describing the distinctions drawn) 'the cornerstone of Austin's doctrine' (Miller 2001: 51). But as Stanley Cavell has pointed out, Austin is not really working up a fundamental opposition between ordinary and fictional utterances: what matters here is the difference between the vision of language as essentially constative advanced by certain philosophical accounts of utterance, and the striking view of the topic made possible by the initial contrast of constative and performative (Cavell 1984: 39–40).

Those who have been inclined to see this exclusion of the non-serious utterance as in some way a cornerstone of the Austinian enterprise have also often been keen to characterise it as *ontological*, as specifying a fundamental difference between the reality of the ordinary utterance and the illusions or unreality of literature (see, for example, Schechner 2002: 111 and Jackson 2004: 3). So the non-serious utterance is understood as a mere imitation of a seriousness that is itself understood as an ontological 'realness'. There have been different ways of making this claim, as we shall see in later chapters, but it is important at this stage to note that it assimilates Austin to a position he does not in fact inhabit. Although he describes literary or fictional or theatrical utterances as 'hollow', or as 'etiolations', or as 'parasitic', he does not contrast them with something called the 'real world', as if their not being serious were a matter of their lacking some kind of ontological substance. Rather, in a crucial but only vaguely specified sense, they do not count as they might do if issued in other circumstances. The question of seriousness, then, is primarily a question of felicity or validity, but of a distinctive kind. This 'sea-change in special circumstances' means that the infelicity of a non-serious performative is not the same as the infelicity of an incomplete marriage ceremony. The failure to take effect does not come about because the procedure has been inappropriately or incorrectly invoked. So telling a non-serious from a serious promise does not involve the same kind of criteria as does telling a serious promise from a serious assertion. That is why they are void in 'a peculiar way', in a manner unlike the infelicities of misfires or abuses.

FROM THE PERFORMATIVE TO THE SPEECH ACT

What Austin describes as 'the preliminary isolation of the performative' (Austin 1975: 4) and its schematic presentation takes up the first four of his lectures. When this formula is first encountered it is not unreasonable to expect that this preliminary isolation will be succeeded by a fuller account; instead, what turns out to be preliminary is the very work of isolation itself. As I noted above, a specific kind of infelicity, the mistake, could be adduced that threatens to blur the contrasting criteria of constative truth or falsity, on the one hand, and performative felicity or infelicity, on the other. And Austin has hitherto insisted that the intelligibility of this contrast is central to the definition and understanding of performative utterances as a *separate class*, not just a kind of statement. In the fifth lecture, though, he methodically begins to put precisely that intelligibility in question:

> Contrast the fact that I am apologizing, which depends on the performative 'I apologize' being happy, with the case of the statement 'John is running', which depends for its truth on its being the fact or case that John is running. But perhaps this contrast is not so sound . . . :

> for, to take statements first, connected with the utterance (constative) 'John is running' is the statement 'I am stating that John is running': and this may depend for its truth on the happiness of 'John is running', just as the truth of 'I am apologizing' depends on the happiness of 'I apologize'.
>
> (Austin 1975: 55)

Austin thus uncovers the fact that even constative utterances lend themselves to assessment in the terms of felicity or infelicity, not in addition to their constative function but in the very process of executing it. We should therefore not be too surprised to learn that what is discernible from this side of the contrast is equally evident from the (apparently) opposite viewpoint:

> To take performatives second: connected with the performative (I presume it is one) 'I warn you that the bull is about to charge' is the fact, if it is one, that the bull is about to charge: if the bull is *not*, then indeed the utterance 'I warn you that the bull is about to charge' is open to criticism. . . . We should not in this case say the warning was void – i.e. that he did not warn but only went through a form of warning – nor that it was insincere: we should feel much more inclined to say the warning was false or (better) mistaken, *as with a statement* [my emphasis]. So that considerations of the happiness and unhappiness type may infect statements (or some statements) and considerations of the type of truth and falsity may infect performatives (or some performatives).
>
> (Austin 1975: 55)

What appears to be happening here is that the border between performatives and constatives is becoming indistinct. We now have both a group of statements whose constative truth seems to involve their performative felicity and a group of acts whose performative felicity seems to involve their constative truth. What is not yet clear is the extent of this middle ground: how many statements or acts can be safely set either side of it?

Austin responds to this breakdown of his primary distinction by exploring whether there are other secure criteria that might determine a 'pure' performative. Firstly, he considers the question of grammatical form: this might seem a promising line of enquiry, given the number of exemplarily performative utterances that take the form of a verb in the first person singular present indicative active ('I bet', 'I promise', 'I name', 'I do'). But he soon finds that this will not work, since there are simply too many grammatical forms that a performative can take (even the monosyllabic exclamation 'Bull!', for example, could be performative in a number of ways: issuing a warning, refusing a claim), and it is anyway easy to argue that the grammatical form most frequently characteristic of the baldest of performative utterances can be deployed in non-performative cases. It could not be demonstrated, in other words, that constative utterances – statements – are not issued in exactly the same grammatical form as performatives: 'I state that it is raining' is grammatically identical to 'I bet that it is raining'. Secondly, he pursues the possibility that it might be possible to deduce a basic grammatical form, the 'explicit performative', encoded within the variety of particular forms taken by the full range of performative utterances. This could then be isolated as the performative in all its purity. But this runs into exactly the same trouble as his first gambit: the pure form that ought, according to his hypothesis, to lie behind or within the grammatical multiplicity of actual performatives cannot be isolated. As Austin says in summary at the end of his seventh lecture:

> We have found . . . that it is often not easy to be sure that, even when it is apparently in explicit form, an utterance is performative or that it is not; and typically anyway, we still have utterances beginning 'I state that . . . ' which seem to satisfy the requirements of being performative, yet which surely are the making of statements, and surely are essentially true or false.
>
> (Austin 1975: 91)

His subsequent declaration that 'it is time to make a new start on the problem' should therefore hardly come as a surprise. The distinction between saying (stating) and doing is to be abandoned; he will instead explore 'the circumstances of "issuing an utterance"' (Austin 1975: 92). If performatives and constatives cannot be properly isolated from each other, the different aspects of language use that the terms denote must be examined together in a focus on the 'speech act' in general.

LOCUTION, ILLOCUTION AND PERLOCUTION

The terminology for this examination is worked out in the eighth lecture. Every utterance or speech act is now to be considered along three axes, each of which denotes a particular element or function of the whole. There is, firstly, the dimension of 'locution', by which Austin means the semantic and referential functions of language. Thus if I say 'there is a bull in the field' I invoke the capacity of the sounds uttered both to stand for the idea of a kind of creature in a particular relation to a kind of terrain, and to mark out this particular creature here as one of the relevant kind. Secondly, we have the 'illocutionary' dimension, which denotes the kind of act I was accomplishing or attempting to accomplish in saying these words: warning, threatening and so on. Since this is a question not of what the utterance means or refers to but of what it is or does, Austin describes it as its illocutionary *force*. Here, the two alternatives of constative and performative have been rethought as distinctive but interdependent aspects of the total speech act.

But he then complicates the picture by adding a third dimension, the 'perlocutionary'. If illocution denotes the function performed *in* saying something, then perlocution denotes the effect I produced *by* issuing the utterance. So, for example, in saying 'there's a bull in that field' I performed the illocutionary act of warning you. At the same time, in saying what I did I also performed a perlocutionary act: I scared you witless, or I made you run away. Both illocution and perlocution describe what we might call the pragmatics of the speech act, the kinds of work in the world that linguistic utterances are able to accomplish in the very process of meaning or referring. The two terms, however, denote a very different sense of the pragmatic: whereas the work of the illocutionary is accomplished in the saying of whatever is said, that of the perlocutionary is more a matter of the contingent consequences or effects that might or might not follow the issuing of a speech act. So when the foreman of the jury says 'Guilty', he or she performs the illocutionary act of declaring the accused guilty. It is done in being said. But we might also expect such a declaration to have perlocutionary effects: by saying 'Guilty', the foreman was able to effect a change in the emotional states and behaviour of many of the people in court. Or, to return to my first example, if I am able to warn you (illocution) that there is a bull in the field, my warning might also serve to persuade you (perlocution) not to jump over the gate. These different functions depend on different conditions for their success, however. If you recognise my warning as a warning, hearing it and taking it in the right way – if, as Austin puts it, I 'secure uptake' – then the act of warning is accomplished. But the same is not true of persuasion: whatever I say, and whatever you understand me to be doing in saying it, it still might not take place. You vault the gate, unpersuaded – but you can't say you weren't warned.

We must be careful not to assume, though, that this way of putting the difference is the same as a claim that the illocutionary work of utterances does not involve consequences or effects. People who find themselves subject to the illocutionary act of being arrested are likely to notice a change in the way they are treated by the police. Indeed, they may well go on to be the focus of the further illocutionary acts of being charged, accused, convicted and sentenced, a chain of acts that are all causally related. But these illocutionary acts, even as they presuppose or enable their neighbours in the chain, are all themselves discrete actions, the enactment of certain conventional procedures or formulae which, in the right conditions and on the right basis, constitute a particular and distinctive event in the world. And they do this *just insofar as* they are properly executed. It is this sense of the pragmatic work of utterances that Austin is trying to isolate in distinguishing the force of illocution from perlocution.

STATEMENTS AS SPEECH ACTS

Having thus anatomised the speech act, Austin returns to the class of utterances with which he began, the constatives or statements wrongly assumed in the 'descriptive fallacy' to be normative for language use in general. How might they be accommodated in this new landscape of the speech act? The answer comes quickly:

> Once we realize that what we have to study is not the sentence but the issuing of an utterance in a speech-situation, there can hardly be any longer a possibility of not seeing that stating is performing an act.
>
> (Austin 1975: 139)

Stating, Austin claims, is to take its place alongside promising, warning, betting, threatening, appointing, naming, declaring, announcing, guaranteeing and the many other kinds of illocutionary acts that we may be doing *in* saying something. As we have already seen, it is not even possible to protest that a special relation of statements to the true/ false criterion can mark them out in their purity, since the issue of correspondence to the facts of a situation is also crucial to the achievement of some kinds of felicity. Approaching the problem from the other side, it is possible to argue that the assessment of the truth or falsity of a statement itself depends on a judgement of the statement's felicity as an illocutionary act:

> Suppose that we confront [the statement that] 'France is hexagonal' with the facts, in this case, I suppose, with France, is it true or false? Well, if you like, up to a point; of course I can see what you mean by saying that it is true for certain intents and purposes. It is good enough for a top-ranking general, perhaps, but not for a geographer. . . . It is essential to realize that 'true' and 'false' . . . do not stand for anything simple at all; but only for a general dimension of being a right or proper thing to say as opposed to a wrong thing, in these circumstances, to this audience, for these purposes and with these intentions.
>
> (Austin 1975: 143, 145)

In this way, assessments even of simple truths seem to require attention to considerations of validity. The different criteria of performative and constative are brought home to each other, and a new vision of 'the total speech-act in the total speech-situation' (Austin 1975: 148) opens up. The initial exploration of the peculiar class of statements that did an action instead of describing it has issued in a focus on speaking as a kind of action.

What, then, is the promise of such a framework? What can it offer, and to whom? The patient, even pedantic exploration of the distinctions that can be drawn in language about language reveals a new way of restoring the activity of saying to the business of doing, and the criterion of procedural or normative correctness or rightness to that of truth-to-fact. It holds out the prospect of tracing the pragmatic structure of our utterances in tracking the network of commitments and responsibilities in which we can engage when speaking. Some of these will take the form of explicit systems or sets of conventions, such as football, chess, judicial or parliamentary procedure, yet the life of such systems will be shown to bear comparison with the implicit or uncertain normativity of the rest of our lives in language. In his final lecture Austin makes a start on this, attempting to formulate a taxonomy of such commitments by separating into different classes the many verbs we use to denote these kinds of linguistic action. What remains unclear, though, is the particular status such an investigation will have: we appear to have strayed onto the territory of linguistics, history, or the social sciences. Yet Austin, when he seeks to place this work in a context of any kind, is clear that it stems from a particular way of practising philosophy, and that its significance needs to be registered in philosophical terms. The next chapter draws out the ways in which both Austin himself and one of his most philosophically significant heirs attempt to make good that claim.

2

PHILOSOPHY AND ORDINARY LANGUAGE
AUSTIN AND CAVELL

> Talking together is acting together, not making motions and noises at
> one another, not transferring unspeakable messages or essences from
> the inside of one closed chamber to the inside of another. The difficul-
> ties of talking together are, rather, *real* ones: the activities we engage
> in by talking are intricate and intricately related to one another.
>
> (Cavell 2002: 33–34)

How To Do Things With Words has often been treated in isolation from
the rest of Austin's work. This is perhaps understandable to some
degree: his collected writings do not take up too much room on the
bookshelves, and his conception of the speech act is their most high pro-
file offering. The problem with reading it alone, though, is that we
inevitably deprive ourselves of any sense of how it is reinforced by
Austin's broader understanding of what philosophy is or should be, and
therefore of any sense of the scope and limits of the conception it outlines. Shorn of this context, it has easily been appropriated by a range of
philosophical projects and a number of other disciplines. But these are

very different kinds of enquiry: they call for very different kinds of evidence or justification, and the knowledge they seek to establish has very different kinds of claim on us. It is therefore important to understand something of the distinctive philosophical approach within which Austin's conception of the performative took shape if we are to get a proper grasp on the transformations visited on that conception by its inheritors.

THE CLAIMS OF THE ORDINARY

Austin's attempt to get past the 'descriptive fallacy' in his Harvard lectures is in fact an exercise in what is customarily described as 'ordinary language philosophy', which is both a helpfully succinct and potentially misleading appellation. His resort to the 'ordinary' as a touchstone for philosophical work is not a thick-headed assertion of common sense, nor a merely dogmatic insistence on the incontrovertibility of a realm of brute facts. Instead, Austin seeks to ground his thinking in a series of claims about how we ordinarily use the very languages that any kind of philosophical project must also invoke as its means, or at least as its starting point. For Austin, the core of any profitable philosophical method had to be the attempt to make explicit the ways in which language was deployed in ordinary usage, '*what we should say when*, and so why and what we should mean by it' (Austin 1979: 181). Thus, his explorations of excuses, or pretending, or of more traditionally philosophical topics such as perception, truth and meaning, were grounded in painstaking attention to the kinds of discriminations that we make when we use the relevant words in appropriate, ordinary ways.

His sense that these discriminations matter derives from his attendant claim that the 'analytic' philosophers of his own day, those who understood philosophy's function as grounded in the logical analysis of language, not only wrenched such terms away from their ordinary uses but did so both incompletely and inconsistently. They sought to purify an ordinary use that they saw as misleading or ambiguous, and thus to remake the language by fiat; yet they also remained committed to that language in the sense that they claimed that their ways of talking were a clarification of something fitfully revealed in its ordinary use. So, for example, they might produce a definition of 'meaning' that rode roughshod over its ordinary usage, yet also claim that their definition matters because this is what the word 'meaning' really means when we use it; or they might produce an account of how we perceive objects which downplays the significance of all the ordinary occasions and interests within which the language of perception is used, while simultaneously presuming that the investigation launched still manages to account for such ordinary usage (Austin 1979: 55–75; Austin 1962). Austin's renewal of the resort to ordinary language, then, took place as a reaction against what he understood as philosophy's abandonment of the complex texture of the everyday life it was at the same time claiming to explain. The knowledge of how we use words is both something we already have, at least in the sense that we know how to talk, and something philosophy has forgotten, or turned its back on, or pronounced seriously inadequate. Austin had distinguished company in this turn to the ordinary: during the 1930s and 1940s Ludwig Wittgenstein began to develop a distinctive and massively influential approach to philosophical labour, an approach that sought to escape from the blind alleys down which philosophy customarily leads us by paying careful attention to the everyday 'form of life' within which we live. Thus, Wittgenstein presents analyses of philosophical problems that show how a certain philosophical picture of an aspect of everyday life is in fact untrue to the very aspect it claims to capture (see Wittgenstein 2001).

A crucial point to grasp here is that neither Wittgenstein nor Austin understood themselves to be interested simply in language. The point of this minute attention to the kind of distinctions we draw in speaking as we do is to better comprehend the world we inhabit, the world that is revealed in our speech. So asking how we use the words we use to excuse ourselves from responsibility for our actions, such as 'unintentional' or 'inadvertent', is a way of finding out both what an excuse is, and beyond that what an action is. Such a procedure has an ancient philosophical pedigree: when Socrates, in Plato's writings, asks his interlocutors to consider what their words mean, he is also asking them to consider what the things they use their words to talk about actually are. As Austin himself put it:

> In view of the prevalence of the slogan 'ordinary language' . . . one thing needs specially emphasizing to counter misunderstandings. When we examine what we should say when, what words we should use in what situations, we are looking again not merely at words (or 'meanings', whatever they may be) but also at the realities we use the words to

talk about: we are using a sharpened awareness of words to sharpen our perception of, though not as the final arbiter of, the phenomena. For this reason I think it might be better to use, for this way of doing philosophy, some less misleading name than those given above – for instance, 'linguistic phenomenology', only that is rather a mouthful.

(Austin 1979: 182)

The concern, then, is with language in the world as a crucial element in the texture of experience, and in studying words we are studying phenomena, the very stuff of our experience. The reference here to 'phenomenology', an influential movement in the alternative, continental philosophical tradition, is both flippant and sincere. From its establishment by the German philosopher Edmund Husserl phenomenology presumed as its starting point the necessity of attending carefully to things as they are experienced, and refused to accept that the inherited philosophical categorisations of experience, and the attendant problems and paradoxes they generated, were adequate to the task. It therefore involved a recasting of, or a new beginning for, philosophy. For Austin to align his own work with this kind of enterprise indicates the extent of his dissent from the dominant understanding of the way in which recent Anglo-American thinking had both set out and confined the philosophical enterprise. As Cavell has argued, 'the clarity Austin seeks in philosophy is to be achieved through mapping the fields of consciousness lit by the occasions of a word, not through analyzing or replacing a given word by others. In this sense, philosophy like his is not "analytical"' (Cavell 2002: 100).

LOGICAL POSITIVISM AND THE SCOPE OF PHILOSOPHY

Yet whether or not this kind of attention to ordinary usage could properly be called philosophy has been disputed. From one perspective, it might seem that the kind of project outlined by Austin ought actually to be called a descriptive linguistics. At the conclusion of one essay, Austin wrote of his investigations as perhaps a herald of 'a true and comprehensive *science of language*', 'cool and well regulated, progressing steadily towards a distant final state' after being thrown off by a 'seminal and tumultuous' philosophy in the same way that a stabilising planet is generated out of the thrashing energy of an 'initial, central sun'

(Austin 1979: 232). If it is to be a science, though, it is not entirely clear what 'science' here denotes: Austin cites mathematics, physics and mathematical logic as precedent examples, so the word might refer both to the kind of empirical knowledge characteristic of the natural, social and human sciences, on the one hand, and to the purer formalisations of certain kinds of rationality, on the other, or even to a combination of the two. If we think of it in these terms, then the resort to the ordinary might be understood as granting a methodological privilege to the business of gathering materials from the world around us, much as the natural and social sciences do. Indeed, in speaking of the sources on which he has drawn in order to elaborate his theory of excuses, Austin singles out not only the dictionary, but also the records of legal proceedings and empirical psychology. The problem with characterising Austin's work in this way, though, is that it manifestly fails to live up to the standards of an empirical science. His one reference to 'field work' specifies that it takes place 'in philosophy' (Austin 1979: 183), which would seem to rule out what ought to be the proper business of data collection, so the question remains: if he is so sure of the importance of the ordinary, of 'what we say when', why is he not out there with a clipboard, a questionnaire, a microphone? Where are the statistical analyses of linguistic data, the graphs and maps showing the distribution of usages, the tentative conclusions that might need revision in the light of further evidence? How can he claim to state authoritatively what we would ordinarily say if he hasn't been outside his college study to find out?

Precisely this kind of challenge to Austin's project was presented by the American philosopher Benson Mates (Mates 1964). In Mates's view, 'ordinary language philosophy' was caught between two stools, trying to use the methods of philosophical reflection to support the claims of an empirical science. To argue his case, Mates pointed to a discrepancy in the claims presented by Austin and by Gilbert Ryle, another Oxford philosopher, regarding how we speak about our responsibility for our actions. Ryle had suggested that an action is only qualified as 'voluntary' if we think there is something morally suspect about it, that we don't as a rule describe normal or standard actions as voluntary or involuntary. Austin had concurred to some degree, but suggested that we might say of a gift that it was made voluntarily, and this would not normally imply anything *morally* fishy about such an action even if it did mark that action as somehow exceptional or peculiar. Thus, for instance, if we asked of someone whether she dressed the way she did voluntarily, it would imply that we thought there was something peculiar or fishy about dressing that way. Both philosophers were seeking to point out that any philosophy of action that started from the assumption that all actions are either voluntary or involuntary would be distorting what we in fact say, and how we in fact understand, what it is to act. But the discrepancy, in Mates's view, deprives either claim of its bite. If two ordinary language philosophers cannot agree on what we say in a set of circumstances, if their intuitions merely rival one another, then what could such intuitions actually be worth? The truth of their claims about what we say hasn't been verified; and the only kind of verification that would count would be that provided by a descriptive linguistics, an account of the facts regarding actual usage. So in order to have anything meaningful to say, Austin and his 'ordinary language' colleagues should become empirical linguists; philosophy should be left to proper philosophers.

Underpinning this kind of critique is the understanding of the nature of philosophical enquiry set out by logical positivist thinkers. One of the clearest statements of this understanding was offered by the English philosopher Alfred Ayer in his 1936 book, *Language, Truth and Logic* (Ayer actually described himself as a 'logical empiricist', but the difference is not relevant to my argument here). For Ayer, meaningful assertions or propositions, of a sort that could well include claims about 'what we say', could be of two kinds. There were, firstly, factual or empirical propositions, claims about the world of our experience, and what marked out meaningful from meaningless propositions of this sort was the criterion of their verifiability. As Ayer put it:

> We say that a sentence is factually significant to any given person, if, and only if, he knows how to verify the proposition which it purports to express – that is, if he knows what observations would lead him, under certain conditions, to accept the proposition as being true, or reject it as being false.
>
> (Ayer 1936: 19–20)

So, the sentence or proposition 'The President of the United States has flat feet' would be an empirical claim; its truth or falsity would be a factual matter, and we would know that we needed to get some evidence regarding the state of the presidential feet in order to verify it. Crucially for Ayer all factual statements about the world, even those that are rather more general in their reference, are also either valid or invalid empirically. So the statement 'all human beings have flat feet', even if it had been uniformly verified by past experience, would also be open to falsification by the same means; it would cease to be true as soon as we found a human being with high arches, an eventuality we couldn't rule out simply because past experience had not thrown up such an individual. No empirical proposition, not even a so-called law of nature, can escape this constraint on its validity. A further consequence of Ayer's position is that only this kind of proposition could be a properly meaningful or significant assertion about the world: the empirical method of the natural sciences was therefore to be championed, and metaphysical claims about the essential nature of the universe, theological claims about the existence of God, ethical claims regarding virtue or the good, were all in their different ways declared unverifiable, and therefore meaningless.

Yet these kinds of empirically verifiable claims were not the only ones capable of being true or false. Such propositions were described as 'synthetic', which is to say that they related different and distinct things to each other in a factual claim. There were also, however, the 'analytic' propositions of philosophy, which could also be meaningful even though they said nothing about the world. A stock example of such a proposition is the sentence 'all bachelors are unmarried'. Now, we would not need to test this empirically, collecting evidence about whether or not all bachelors were indeed unmarried. It is true necessarily, *a priori* or without any reference to experience, just as 'some bachelors are married' is false in the same way. If such propositions are necessarily true it is because they are tautologies, and to deny them is to attempt to occupy the untenable ground of self-contradiction. Without checking anything in the world we can tell that 'all bachelors are unmarried' must be true, simply because to maintain the opposite makes no sense. All bachelors *must be* unmarried, because 'being unmarried' is part of what 'bachelor' means. Ayer maintained that all the truths of logic and mathematics were tautologous in precisely this way. They could not be confuted by experience, and therefore were necessarily true; but the price for achieving this apparently elevated status was that they did not make any assertion about the world as such. Analytical truths registered the logical consistency of a conventional system.

The job of philosophy, in Ayer's view, was therefore to perform some logical straightening out of the knotted business of our claims to knowledge, as well as clarifying the precise relationship between logical truths and the factual knowledge of science. Meaningful sentences needed to be carefully divided from the meaningless, and the former needed to be sorted into analytic and synthetic. The language in which all such propositions were stated needed itself to be sorted out, so that the truth-telling functions it was seeking to express could be properly clarified. For example, our natural language might mislead us into thinking that the statement 'He is the author of that book' is logically identical with 'A cat is a mammal', even though the 'is' in each statement is performing a very different logical function (Ayer 1936: 72). Similarly, the fact that the assertions 'John exists' and 'John laughs' are grammatically identical might lead us to imagine that the same kind of claim is being entered, when in fact this is not the case. So, through the work of analysing sentences, translating them into logically equivalent sentences in order to clarify them, philosophy makes explicit the logical relationships both captured and obscured by ordinary language.

An interesting point to note, though, is Ayer's account of how we come upon the analytic truths we recognise as necessary. We are not born with them, of course; rather, we learn them through experience, and in particular through learning the language we actually speak. The crucial part of this process of learning, though, is the recognition that such truths 'do not owe their validity to empirical verification. . . . Once we have apprehended them we see that they are necessarily true, that they hold good for every conceivable instance' (Ayer 1936: 95–96). The risk associated with acknowledging that we learn these truths empirically, though, is that we might be brought to think just 'that philosophy tells us how certain symbols are actually used'. This would suggest that 'the propositions of philosophy are factual propositions concerning the behaviour of a certain group of people; and this is not the case' (Ayer 1936: 86). It is because the conventions encode logical relations that a language can bear necessary truths; deducing what a certain sentence logically entails is what philosophy does, 'and it is in this logical activity, and not in any empirical study of the linguistic habits of any group of people, that philosophical analysis consists' (Ayer 1936: 86–87).

STANLEY CAVELL: THE NECESSARY TRUTHS OF ORDINARY LANGUAGE PHILOSOPHY

From this perspective, then, Mates's accusations against ordinary language philosophy might seem clear and well-founded. Austin's claims about ordinary language were factual or empirical, and their truth, could it be established, would therefore be contingent rather than necessary. Such claims were therefore indubitably scientific rather than philosophical: Austin and company were in the wrong business. Unsurprisingly, such a dismissal provoked a response, though from Stanley Cavell rather than Austin, in an essay entitled 'Must We Mean What We Say?'. Cavell sought to show that the logical positivist account of philosophy was lacking; that it was consequently incapable of registering the claims of the ordinary language approach. Such claims, Cavell argued, were not to be categorised as empirical in the sense meant by both Mates and Ayer. If a claim such as 'when we describe an action as voluntary we imply that there is something funny about it' was true, its truth was not merely a matter of correctly describing an empirical situation. Certainly, such a claim could not be reduced to a relation of logical equivalence; consequently, one could not say that its truth was just a matter of avoiding self-contradiction. Neither could it be made without some reference beyond logic to the world, to the pragmatic consideration of language in use. In fact, since it precisely marked the circumstances in which something was the proper thing to say, it had to involve understanding language as more than a system of meanings that could be logically related to one another.

Despite all this, Cavell insisted, such claims were not just factual propositions concerning the behaviour of a group of people. Instead, they did not describe patterns or regularities in the way a community used its language; rather, they articulated *from the inside* something of the principles governing the language *we* speak, principles that do not quite take the form of properly logical relations but, as principles, are essential to the business of using language and therefore of inhabiting our world. They are not empirically verifiable propositions; instead, they articulate the norms of the language within which, and only within which, we can even begin to construct such propositions. In other words, an ordinary language approach is not in the end concerned to report what we mean by what we say as if that were simply a matter of fact; instead it focuses attention on what we *must mean* when we say whatever we do, on the not obviously logical necessities that structure language use. To attend to ordinary language in the way that Austin did, to seek to produce the kinds of claims about ordinary language that characterised his work, was therefore to be engaged in the business of 'uncovering the necessary conditions of the shared world' (Cavell 2002: xx). Such activity could not just accept the simple way in which Ayer and likeminded thinkers had tried to separate philosophy from empirical science, on the one hand, and from metaphysics or mere nonsense on the other. Thus Austin, in Cavell's reading, explores a realm of philosophical interest that logical positivism had completely occluded.

The evidence for such claims regarding the non-logical or non-analytic necessities of what we say is therefore not something we have to go out and gather from the world, as a descriptive linguist might. Instead, we acquire it in much the same way as Ayer says we acquire the principles of logic, through our acquisition of our native languages. As Cavell says, '*learning what these implications are is part of learning the language*; no less a part than learning its syntax, or learning what it is to which terms apply: they are an essential part of what we communicate when we talk' (Cavell 2002: 11–12). Crucially, Cavell is not talking here about the acquisition of a second language, someone else's language, a language we don't yet know. What is in question here is *our own* language. We already have the evidence for what we would ordinarily say in a particular situation, by virtue of being native speakers of a language: we are, in fact, its source. Ordinary language is not out there somewhere: it is *here*, in the study, too, or the seminar room, and here because we speak it, because we speak at all. To ask how our own language is used I ask not what *those people* (over there) say, but what *we* say, and in so doing I strive to articulate the principles I implicitly invoke in speaking the language I speak. If Ryle and Austin disagree about the situations in which the word 'voluntary' could ordinarily be applied, if they differ on the necessary pragmatic implications of describing an action as 'voluntary', then that need not mean that there is no underlying principle for such application, and that we have nothing to go on here but the bald intuition or anecdotal evidence of the philosopher. In trying to resolve any such disagreement we might seek to put pressure on the claim of each, to see whether it works. But in doing so, we will be appealing precisely to standards of correctness or appropriateness, to the principles or pragmatic grammar of ordinary language. Making such principles explicit may not be an easy business, always, but one way to begin the task is to imagine and examine exemplary situations in which we use the word, that is by recalling 'what we should say when'. In examining such situations, though, the philosopher is attending to examples rather than to samples. Ordinary usage is therefore not an aggregate of individual appellations; it is the very attunement in signification that gives us language in the first place, and that enables us to have a shared world in which to live. So I cannot use words to mean whatever I choose without becoming unintelligible, without in some sense ceasing to speak: when I articulate the pragmatic significance of the word 'voluntary', for example, I am spelling out what *must* be meant in using it, what 'voluntary' means pragmatically, not what I wish to mean by it. Insofar as we are language users, therefore, and not insofar as we are experts in empirical linguistics, we are equipped to test and register the validity of claims about 'what we say when'.

RULES, NECESSITY AND NORMATIVITY

In this essay, then, Cavell suggests that the propositions of the ordinary language philosopher claim to articulate the pragmatic rules or criteria that structure our lives in language. Ordinary language is therefore normative for us, its speakers: to say anything at all is to be open to considerations of correctness or validity. If there are rules of this sort, though, they are not necessarily prescriptions for how we *ought* to speak, either moral or other kinds of injunctions. Rather, they are more closely akin to, though not necessarily exactly like, the rules of a game or some other social institution: speaking just depends upon the rules of ordinary language if it is to be done, just as a game of chess depends upon the rules of chess if it is to take place. Two people might well sit across a chequered board from each other, and even move what we would call chess pieces around in a regular fashion; but this would not be a game of chess unless it invoked the rules of chess. Once such rules had been invoked, though, one could not simply move the pieces around however one wished, even if one moved them in some kind of pattern. Now, there would be rules that governed how the pieces *could* move (Cavell 2002: 25–31). Such rules might therefore be understood as constitutive: they make up or constitute the practice, whether it is a game like chess or something less clearly particular, such as language.

We need to be careful here, though, in talking about 'constitutive rules' in this way. Cavell does not claim that the necessity invoked is in some way securely metaphysical, a singular, fundamental claim about the world as a whole. Neither he nor Austin seek this kind of security, and the search for any kind of ultimate, generalisable foundation would strike them as a paradigmatic instance of the temptation to which philosophy is particularly prone, its dissatisfaction with the kinds of necessity or certainty with which we ordinarily live. The principles to which they seek to draw us back can only be those that are immanent in a particular language at a particular time. A particular realm of rules or practices will not hold for all times and places, and could probably have been otherwise than it is. As Cavell argues:

> It is perfectly true that English might have developed differently than it has and therefore have imposed different categories on the world than it does; and if so, it would have enabled us to assert, describe, question, define, promise, appeal, etc., in ways other than we do. But using English now – to converse with others in the language, or to understand the world, or to think by ourselves – means knowing which forms in what contexts are normative for performing the activities we perform by using the language.

> (Cavell 2002: 33)

These necessities are historically specific, culturally finite; they have fissures or borders, however those are to be imagined. At the same time, however, it is not possible to imagine a shared world, a world given in language, without such normative principles. While ours may be finite, some such principles will always be required wherever language is spoken.

There are other reasons, too, why to talk here of constitutive rules could be at least a bit misleading. It might lead us, for example, to imagine that they are written down somewhere, or are the product of explicit agreements, or furnish us with an exhaustive calculus or set of algorithmic procedures. But we cannot point to an original constitution, a founding document or book of laws, for ordinary language. In its absence, there would appear to be nothing fundamental that underpins or guarantees the continuation or preservation of a shared world, and nothing to forestall the possibility of conflict or difference across it. For this reason, the analogy of language with codified games like chess, or with institutions predicated on procedural rules, should not be pushed too far. Nor should it be assumed that any such rules are on a level with even the basic algorithmic rules for generating mathematical series. And if there can be no such systematisation, can it make sense to argue that the principles or criteria with which ordinary language furnishes us can accurately be described as a set of rules? Complementing his reading of Austin with an exploration of the ways in which the later Wittgenstein tackles such questions, Cavell suggests not (see Cavell 2002: 44–96; see also Affeldt 1998, Mulhall 2003). But surely accepting this means that any claim to the effect that language use involved an implicit level of normative necessity, an appeal to criteria that determine appropriateness or correctness, is utterly undermined?

Cavell's answer to this challenge gestures towards the kind of limits to philosophical justification that such an objection appears to overlook, while also querying the understanding of necessity it presumes. He points out that we do in fact combine both an invocation of linguistic standards of validity or correctness, standards which are therefore normative for us, with an incapacity to inscribe such standards finally as a system of rules or an ultimate foundation that therefore could insulate them from challenge, change or damage. As he puts it:

> We learn and teach words in certain contexts, and then we are expected, and expect others, to be able to project them into further contexts. Nothing insures that this projection will take place (in particular, not the grasping of universals nor the grasping of books of rules), just as nothing insures that we will make, and understand, the same projections. That on the whole we do is a matter of our sharing routes of interest and feeling, modes of response, senses of humor and of significance and of fulfillment, of what is outrageous, of what is similar to what else, what a rebuke, what forgiveness, of when an utterance is an assertion, when an appeal, when an explanation – all the whirl of organism Wittgenstein calls 'forms of life.' Human speech and activity, sanity and community, rest upon nothing more, but nothing less, than this. It is a vision as simple as it is difficult, and as difficult as it is (and because it is) terrifying.
>
> (Cavell 2002: 52)

The necessity or normativity of ordinary language, therefore, is vulnerable: it is an agreement in signification, an attunement, that depends on our maintaining it in our various communities, our practices of learning and teaching, our ways of being together. If this kind of normativity does not seem rigorous enough to the philosopher, then that in the end is his or her problem. Lives in language will go on, whether or not they can be justified to the philosopher's satisfaction: in looking for more than can be furnished, such an enquirer will miss the weight or density of what is actually there.

SPEECH ACTS AND LINGUISTIC NORMATIVITY

How, then, does Austin's exposition of the performative utterance fit into this picture of ordinary language? Given its development of a technical vocabulary for describing the general characteristics of the speech act, this exposition might seem to be a rather more methodical effort at system-building than the kinds of investigation highlighted in Cavell's account of ordinary language philosophy. But it is also worked out of a consideration of 'what we say when', asking for example what we mean or imply when we say 'I promise' or 'I know', and taking its bearings from the result of such enquiries. What it in the end suggests is that the exploration of such aspects of our language provides a more carefully honed awareness of the normativity of language in use, of how certain forms in certain contexts 'are normative for performing the activities we perform by using the language', as Cavell put it in the passage quoted above. The suggestion that language has an irreducible illocutionary dimension, that utterances are always open to assessment in terms of their felicity or correctness, therefore serves to reinforce or make explicit the view of language as part of the pragmatic matrix of everyday life that emerges from the approach Austin pursued throughout his career. This general sense is then itself reinforced through the specific analysis of such linguistic possibilities as promising, ordering, betting and so on.

The rules or conditions for the felicity of the speech act that Austin examines in his Harvard lectures are thus themselves articulations of the normativity inherent in speaking. This is a general point that is implicitly pursued throughout the lectures, but it is also something that Austin on occasion handles explicitly. In an early essay, 'The Meaning of a Word', he had attempted to account for the philosopher's sense that some propositions or statements might convey a necessity that was not simply analytic or tautological by drawing attention to the ways in which the consideration of use might be relevant (Austin 1979: 62–69). Among the examples he drew on there was a somewhat peculiar statement known as 'Moore's paradox' after its author, the English philosopher G. E. Moore: 'The cat is on the mat but I do not believe it is'. This was a perennial object of philosophical curiosity, pondered by Wittgenstein in his *Philosophical Investigations* (Wittgenstein 2001: 162e–64e), and deemed problematic in being apparently logically acceptable even though patently absurd. In Lecture Four of *How To Do Things With Words*, at precisely the point where he is beginning to complicate his preliminary distinction between the performative and the constative, Austin returns to Moore's paradox (and the equivalently troubling 'All Jack's children are bald but Jack has no children') in order to uncover 'how many ways, and why, they outrage speech, and wherein the outrage lies' (Austin 1975: 48). His answer is to point to their transgression of the felicity conditions he had suggested for illocutionary acts:

> Suppose I did say 'the cat is on the mat' when it is not the case that I believe the cat is on the mat, what should we say? Clearly it is a case of *insincerity*. In other words: the unhappiness here is, though affecting a statement, exactly the same as the unhappiness infecting 'I promise . . . ' when I do not intend, do not believe, &c. The insincerity of an assertion is the same as the insincerity of a promise, since both promising and asserting are procedures intended for use by persons having certain thoughts. . . . What is to be said of the statement that 'John's [sic] children are all bald' if made when John has no children? . . . Here I shall say 'the utterance is void'. . . . In order to explain what can go wrong with statements we cannot just concentrate on the proposition involved (whatever that is) as has been done traditionally. We must consider the total situation in which the utterance is issued.
>
> (Austin 1975: 50–52)

We cannot properly assert that 'the cat is on the mat', in other words, without implying that we believe this state of affairs to be the case. To deny this pragmatic implication may not be to outrage logic, but it is to set one's face against the normativity in our use of language. Asserting something just carries the implication of belief: in another essay, Austin suggested that an assertion was like a promise in committing us in this fashion (Austin 1979: 98–103). Moore's paradox therefore offends not against logic but against the normative conditions of ordinary language in use: the 'paradox' is dissolved if we recall the general point that language necessarily involves this pragmatic or illocutionary dimension, and the specific observation that the local grammar of asserting something – what we must mean when we utter 'I assert that . . . ' or an analogous expression – involves this implied commitment to belief.

WORDS AND BONDS

Austin's sense, then, of the pragmatic implications of 'what we say when' is here complemented by a more concentrated examination of how we talk about the kinds of linguistic action in which we engage. His whole approach works to reveal how speaking is a matter of operating within a normative framework of responsibilities and entitlements, of implications to which we are committed in saying what we say. Looking carefully at what we mean when we say 'I promise', or 'I assert that . . . ' therefore allows us to make such commitments clear from another standpoint, and comparing these and other kinds of speech act suggests that we might be able to clarify the ways in which speaking is doing something at a more general level. The Harvard lectures thus address in a different fashion the questions regarding the performance of *actions* that Austin continued to explore elsewhere. In a series of lectures, seminars and articles, most prominently 'A Plea for Excuses', 'Pretending' and the posthumously published 'Three Ways of Spilling Ink', Austin dwelled at length on the ways in which we ordinarily discriminate between, for example, an action done 'automatically' and one done 'inadvertently', and the differences between doing something 'intentionally', 'deliberately', or 'on purpose' (see Austin 1979). His concern in developing these analyses was to show what our ordinary understanding of action might be, through making explicit precisely the ways in which we think an action may be excused, or compromised, or otherwise said to have gone wrong (Austin 1979: 271).

Intriguingly, though, setting this consideration of action alongside his investigation of how we talk about speaking did not necessarily suggest that speaking could simply be seen as a species of action like any other, as one particular passage from *How To Do Things With Words* shows (see Cavell 1994: 53–128, Hill 1984, Miller 2001: 30–34). At the end of his first lecture Austin offers an emphatic endorsement of the 'plain saying' that '*our word is our bond*', declaring that it is supported by 'accuracy and morality alike' (Austin 1975: 10). As we saw above, this endorsement comes as a rebuttal of the claim that the words we say do not count as the performance of acts themselves, but are merely outward reports of inward, spiritual performances – so that when someone says 'I promise . . . ' he or she is doing no more than reporting, constatively, that an inner promise has been undertaken. In Austin's eyes this is inaccurate, precisely because a promise is made in being said: declaring later that you didn't mean it, that you didn't enact it inwardly, that you never intended to keep it, will not relieve you of the necessary pragmatic implications of your utterance, the commitment you entered into in speaking. A false promise is still a promise, though ever so unhappy. It is an abuse, not a misfire (Austin 1975: 9).

In the same sentence that invokes accuracy, though, we also have the invocation of morality. The temptation here is to cast 'the plain saying' as something like an imperative: 'our word is our bond' would therefore be equivalent to 'we ought to mean what we say'. But this cannot be quite right, because Austin is not maintaining that we ought to make our word our bond, that we ought to live up to our commitments, or any other such injunction. Instead he is saying that in speaking we are, simply, subject to such linguistic necessities: in this situation we do not have the choice between 'meaning it' and 'not meaning it' that would make a claim that we 'ought' to do one or the other properly intelligible. This is the sense in which, as Cavell says, we *must* mean what we say. At the same time, Austin's attempts in 'A Plea for Excuses' and 'Three Ways of Spilling Ink' to clarify all the ways in which acts might be done involuntarily, accidentally, mistakenly, inadvertently, unintentionally, and so on, have furnished him with an elaborate map of the ways in which we might be able to disavow the acts we have done. Acts, therefore, are precisely the kind of thing that can at least be open to mitigation or excuse in precisely this fashion. But although actions can be done inadvertently, accidentally, or mistakenly, it is not obvious that speaking can always be open to this kind of mitigation. Insofar as our language gives us our world, our lives must be lived in language.

Perhaps, then, illocutionary acts are not to be disavowed or excused in the same way as other actions: perhaps you cannot keep yourself back from your words, and therefore manage not to be responsible for and answerable to them. The implication of this, Cavell suggests,

> is that the saying of words is not excusable the way the performance of actions is; or, in a word, that saying something is after all, or before all, on Austinian grounds, not exactly or merely or transparently doing something.
>
> (Cavell 1994: 104–5)

Speaking, that is to say, is not quite the kind of act that the language of disavowed responsibility appropriate for other actions might easily address. Instead, our speech acts tether or bind us to our words in a way that is not always open to the prospect either of disavowal or of excuse. In this way, too, they testify to the necessities of our lives in ordinary language.

ETHICS, POLITICS AND ORDINARY LANGUAGE

To talk in this way of morality, and of bonds, suggests an ethical or a political dimension to ordinary language philosophy. Yet the picture that emerges from such considerations is potentially a troubling one. If our utterances situate us within a matrix of commitments or demands, such that giving a promise to someone, say, changes our status in relation to that person and submits us to the responsibilities of a promise, to the obligation to mean it and keep it, then we might be tempted to think of these bonds as duties to which we cannot help but be subject. Our language would then appear to us as a kind of law, a set of principles that governed the way we could speak and act. To speak of the normativity of language in this way would be to consider these rules or conventions as imposed upon us. We could not *own* such commitments as this; they would be given to us in the way that the rules of football determine the obligations and options of its players for as long as they are on the pitch. The difference with language here, of course, is that we could never actually step out of it the way we can step off the football field. Language in this model would be a set of rules or conventions that we would be powerless to refuse; but at the same time, in describing them as conventions or agreements, or in terms of games, other connotations would be invoked.

In this picture, the political shape of our linguistic life recalls some of the complications surrounding the myth of the 'social contract', a myth that dominates the social and political philosophy of early modern thinkers such as Thomas Hobbes, John Locke and Jean-Jacques Rousseau. For such thinkers, a system of social roles – obligations and rights – is legitimised if it can be claimed that it is founded on an original agreement that binds all contracting parties. Where consent to any such agreement could not be shown to have taken place, it could be argued that it was implicit in the conduct of those living peaceably within the society concerned and benefiting from the security and opportunities it offered. Yet this idea of 'tacit consent' could be attacked as a sleight of hand designed to obscure the lack of any power held by those living within a society actually to give their consent to it, and thus as a way of claiming contractual legitimation for a system of social obligations that did not actually have a genuinely contractual basis; in such situations, the notion that any such society could be legitimised through the appeal to a contract to which all those bound by its terms had somehow consented could be exposed as illusory.

Is, then, the appeal to notions of agreement or convention in ordinary language philosophy equally compromised? Does such talk add a veneer of political legitimacy to a system of illocutionary commitments or duties that cannot or should not be justified in this fashion? We could hardly claim, surely, that the ordinary language through which we live is not penetrated by or complicit with unequal power relations, relations that accomplish the oppression or silencing of certain social groups. Slavery happened in ordinary language; so did fascism; so, too, do racism, sexism and homophobia. If we cannot help but speak the language of the society within which we find ourselves, then surely such speaking should not be taken as an indication of our consent to the commitments it requires of us? Is this talk of the binding force of our agreement in language not therefore simply an ideological fig leaf that conceals such non-consensual aspects of what it is to be subjected to, and in, language? In such circumstances, the ordinary language philosopher who talks of *morality* when referring to our illocutionary commitments might well seem to be the mystificatory, conservative figure outlined by J. Hillis Miller (Miller 2001: 56–58, and see the

Introduction), insisting deceptively on the contractual basis, and there-fore on the moral and political legitimacy, of inequitable linguistic com-munities.

Such a conclusion, however, does not necessarily follow from the con-sideration of the ethical and political implications of Austin's thinking on performativity. He does in fact invoke the social contract in his account of the speech act, though without suggesting that it offers a simple analogy for the illocutionary necessities of language (Austin 1975: 28–29). Cavell, too, has recalled the notion in further attempts to clarify his picture of ordinary language, and such clarification offers fuller grounds for suggesting that the version of our commitments out-lined in my previous paragraphs is in need of urgent modification (Cavell 1979: 22–28). If the kind of bond to which ordinary language philosophy pointed was simply a constitutive rule or law, then the propositions such a philosophy produced would aim to make explicit the various articles or clauses of this law. To outline 'what we say when', or to insist on the non-logical necessities at work in our use of language, would be to call us back to duties we were perhaps in danger of forget-ting even as we were involved in them. Ordinary language philosophers would thus be taking it upon themselves to remind us of the impersonal and implacable law to which we were unfailingly subject; to speak of such a law as in any way contractual would be to commit precisely the mystificatory or ideological move.

But as we have seen, the investigation of ordinary language does not necessarily furnish us with this kind of knowledge. We may find that asking ourselves what the pragmatic implications of a word such as 'vol-untary' are, for example, or how the pragmatics of stating, ordering or querying are to be understood, does not simply present us with a simple answer. When I make a claim to articulate what 'we' must mean when we say something, I am indeed making a claim to speak for 'us', for a community or a shared world; I am indeed seeking to draw out the extent of 'our' agreement in language use, and therefore to elucidate the normativity of our lives in language. What I don't yet know, though, when I do this, is the extent of the community for which I am claiming to speak. It is always possible, as I suggested above, that my claim may not meet with acceptance. As Cavell says, when the ordinary language philosopher finds a claim such as this rebuffed, 'he hasn't said some-thing false about "us"; he has learned that there is no us (yet, maybe never) to say anything about. What is wrong with his statement is that he made it to the wrong party' (Cavell 1979: 19–20). Particular appeals to norms of the sort that Austin and Cavell both offer might always be refused, or find no echo, or be the occasion for dispute. Crucially, Cavell's insistence that the normativity of language is not anchored in an impersonal matrix of rules ensures that the picture of speaking that emerges from his account is not one of subjection to an implacable linguistic order set over and against us. Instead, for Cavell the commonality of the ordinary is always in process, always up for discussion, always vulnerable precisely to those, philosophers and politicians alike, who feel the need to insist upon an image of linguistic communities as grounded finally in the firm foundations of an impersonal system. For Cavell, then, the claim to articulate the normativity of the ordinary cannot be played as a trump card to put a stop to discussion or preclude dissent. It is for this reason, as the philosopher Jay Bernstein argues in an important essay, that the philosophical appeal to the ordinary should be seen neither as 'a comforting picture' nor as a conservative vision, 'one that imagines the philosopher as the voice of traditional wisdom in a traditional society' (Bernstein 2003: 116).

If this is the case, then the person who claims to articulate what we mean when we say something is not setting before us the tablets of the law, like Moses presenting the Israelites with the Ten Commandments or a metaphysician presenting us with knowledge of ultimate grounds. These are instead instances where someone undertakes to speak both for him or herself and for others, for a community of equals:

> not as a parent speaks for you, i.e., instead of you, but as someone in mutuality speaks for you, i.e., speaks your mind. Who these others are, for whom you speak and by whom you are spoken for, is not known a priori, though it is in practice generally treated as given. To speak for yourself then means risking the rebuff – on some occasion, perhaps once for all – of those for whom you claimed to be speaking; and it means risking having to rebuff – on some occasion, perhaps once for all – those who claimed to be speaking for you.
>
> (Cavell 1979: 27)

The ordinary language philosopher does not claim, therefore, to articulate a view from nowhere, before or beyond the pragmatic matrix of our linguistic lives. It is in this sense that the scene in which claims about ordinary language are issued and considered is itself a political or ethical scene. Such a vision offers a particular sense, too, of what such a scene involves: an ethical openness to other voices, and a democratic and liberal insistence on the importance and difficulty of speaking representatively. It is therefore one in which we take responsibility for our shared world, and thus explore its outlines, its limits and its possibilities. Should we find ourselves in community, then that is not the end of the matter: we would not all be speaking with one voice. Under such conditions, a modified idea of the social contract might reasonably be recalled. In claiming that such a world is ours, I am recognising both that it is mine and that I belong to it; in taking responsibility for it, I am reaffirming my consent to it and hoping that it meets with yours. The mode of agreement outlined in this scene is not one that invokes an original agreement or contract to set up a society; it instead appeals to an agreement *in* acting together that cannot simply be translated into the authorisation of a prior law or set of rules. This scene is therefore one in which the work of recognising 'our' commitments by exploring the necessities of 'our' language use is always inhabited by the responsibility of speaking for the community within which such necessities might hold, and the ever-present possibility that what I say will find no echoing affirmation from those I address, or a dissenting affirmation that is also a challenge. For these reasons, if our words are our bonds they are not simply fetters: such bonds can also be a form of mutuality that may need both cultivation and protection.

3

A GENERAL THEORY OF SPEECH ACTS

SEARLE

We are in the position of someone who has learned to play chess without ever having the rules formulated and who wants such a formulation.

(Searle 1969: 55)

Through exploring the work of Austin and Cavell we have followed both the basic elaboration of the category of the performative or speech act, and some of the ways in which such a category might be set within the context of a broader philosophical resort to, or picture of, the pragmatic matrix of language in use. In the last chapter, I traced out the challenges that faced the claim that language is fundamentally normative, challenges that issued in specifically political or moral questions. Underpinning such questions was the more basic question of whether such normativity is to be accounted for through the model of an impersonal system of rules, or whether it admits of other constructions. For Cavell, as we saw, the fruitful emphasis is on the latter possibility; but his is not the only nor even the most influential attempt to develop a philosophical picture of linguistic normativity out of the work of Austin. In this chapter, I will set out how the American philosopher John Searle, another pupil of Austin, built an account of the speech act marked by very different assumptions, emphases and implications. Although it has often been suggested, not least by Searle himself, that his is essentially an elaboration or completion of Austin's work, this suggestion is likely to mislead. In taking over, rewriting and extending Austin's investigations, Searle introduced modifications that served to reconfigure central elements in the conceptual architecture, and are in many ways as contentious or problematic as they are influential.

UNIVERSAL PRAGMATICS

Regardless of Austin's own sense of his philosophical project, or indeed of Cavell's reading of that project, those who picked up his work on speech acts were often most clearly impressed by its potential to furnish precisely a systematic basis for the thinking of language in action. It would be foolish to deny that there is plenty in Austin's outline of the pragmatics of utterance to give encouragement to such ways of reading him. His tripartite division of the speech act into locution, illocution and perlocution, and his claim that illocution is a matter of conformity to rules or conventions, could quite easily be taken as an invitation to look for a truly systematic basis, a fundamental *grammar*, underlying the speech situation. One thinker who has sought to develop this aspect of the concept of the speech act is the German philosopher Jürgen Habermas. The intellectual tradition from which Habermas took his bearings had come to understand the very structure of rationality itself as implicated in the kinds of violence and domination that characterised Nazism (see Adorno and Horkheimer 1972). Philosophy thus seemed to offer little chance of working out a basis on which the business of making and justifying ethical and political claims could be rescued from such debilitating implications. At the same time, the thinking of action was also in difficulty: philosophical models of human agency as the pursuit of success or of selfish interests appeared to offer little chance for finding something other than the exertion of individual and competing powers in the social world we inhabit.

In the picture of linguistic action developed by Austin, though, Habermas discerned a resource for rescuing the possibility of a rational, non-dominative morality and politics. Like his compatriot Karl-Otto Apel (see Apel 1991, 1998), he discerned in the Austinian exploration of the pragmatics of the speech situation a necessarily presupposed orientation to communication, to agreements in understanding, even in uses of language that appear to be pursuing selfish strategic ends. By pursuing the rational reconstruction of the general structure of the speech act, Habermas hoped to show that what was fundamental to language use was the basic structure, the necessary conditions, of valid communication: any linguistic action, in other words, presupposed that such conditions were operative, even if they were buried under the distorting weight of strategic or instrumental considerations and social structures. The elaboration of this foundation then allowed Habermas to suggest that the communicative rationality he had outlined offered a means of establishing and justifying genuinely universal claims to moral rightness (see Habermas 1984 & 1987, 1999). Like Cavell, then, he understood that the picture of the speech act might harbour ethical and political promise; unlike Cavell, however, he hoped ultimately to rescue or realise traditional philosophical aspirations to put claims to moral validity on a systematic foundation.

BEYOND ORDINARY LANGUAGE

For Habermas, the notion of the speech act provided a springboard for a philosophical project that built on many other sources, and quickly translated and altered Austinian terms in order to outline very different philosophical claims. Searle, on the other hand, tracked Austin's work more closely even as he remoulded its account of the performative to fit his own purposes. In *Speech Acts: an Essay in the Philosophy of Language* (Searle 1969) and the essays subsequently gathered together in *Expression and Meaning: Studies in the Theory of Speech Acts* (Searle 1979), he set out his fundamental reorganisation of the Austinian inheritance. While accepting and reiterating the basic pragmatic standpoint that 'all linguistic communication involves linguistic acts', and that 'the unit of linguistic communication is not, as has been generally supposed, the symbol, word or sentence, . . . but rather the production or issuance of the symbol or word or sentence in the performance of the speech act' (Searle 1969: 16), he suggested that there was still much to do if the promise of the pragmatic turn was to be made good. In fact, he perceived more broadly that much of the ordinary language philosophy of what he called 'the classical period of linguistic analysis, the period roughly from the end of the second world war until the early sixties' had suffered from a common 'failure to base particular linguistic analyses on any coherent general approach to or theory of language'. Such philosophers had shown 'a nice ear for linguistic nuances and distinctions but little or no theoretical machinery for handling the facts of linguistic distinctions once discovered' (Searle 1969: 131). One of the problems, according to Searle, was that the analysis of how language is used had not taken enough notice of the deeper structural mechanisms underpinning such use. Saying, for example, that the word 'good' is used to commend something flags up the pragmatic dimension of language but tells us nothing about how such a use can come about (Searle 1969: 148–49). The turn away from theories of language and meaning that had no space for the pragmatic, in other words, could not be much of a forward move unless the underlying structure of the pragmatic dimension, the ways in which use was systematically enabled and determined, could be set out.

Crucially, then, Searle was disputing aspects of the ordinary language approach as pursued by Austin and justified by Cavell. But his differences from this approach in fact extend further than arguing that it is insufficiently systematic. Seeking to clarify the concept of action, he rejects the Austinian principle that such clarification requires attention to 'what we say when' we speak of actions. In fact, precisely the opposite is required. Austin, as we saw in the last chapter, suggested that it made no sense for philosophers to suggest that all actions were either voluntary or involuntary, when actions in normal circumstances were not so qualified. To say that an action was done 'voluntarily' would therefore ordinarily be to imply that there was something peculiar or unusual about it, and the philosophical anatomy of the concept of action ignored these pragmatic implications at its peril. Searle disagrees: the reason we do not qualify our unexceptional actions in this way is that we just assume that they are in fact voluntary, and do not need continually to reiterate this apparently obvious point. Paying Austinian degrees of attention to 'what we say when' could therefore be highly misleading; it could well conceal, rather than illuminate, the ways in which our concepts map our world, leading us in this case to dispute the association between normal actions and volition upon which Searle wishes to insist (Searle 1969: 142–46). Philosophical enquiry should therefore not look to the invocation of ordinary language to show us the necessary conditions of our shared world; that world can best be grasped by ignoring the deceptive sign-posting on which Austin and Cavell suggest we should focus. The philosophical promise held out by the notion of linguistic performativity, in other words, can only be made good if it does indeed issue in the wholeness and coherence of a system or calculus of rules.

THE THEORY OF SPEECH ACTS: CONSTITUTIVE CONDITIONS

For Searle, Austin's move into the explicit investigation of utterance in *How To Do Things With Words* seemed to offer an opening for the right kind of systematic work. The exploitation of this opening required Searle to build up a new picture of four conditions central to the successful performance of the speech act that could take the place of Austin's own set of six criteria. Firstly, he specified a 'propositional content condition', a requirement that speech acts contain semantic and referential elements that ensure that they are *about* something. The same content can be found in different kinds of speech act: the order 'shut that door!' has the same propositional content as the question 'Have you shut that door?'. But different kinds of speech acts place different limits on this condition. A promise, for instance, needs its propositional content in the future tense: one cannot promise to do something last year. Secondly, Searle specified 'preparatory conditions', the circumstances that must obtain if an act is to be undertaken successfully. I cannot order you to do something if I lack the status to do so, and I cannot (felicitously) congratulate you on failing your driving test, commiserate with you for winning the lottery, or greet you if we are already in the middle of an intense, face-to-face conversation. The third condition Searle called the 'sincerity condition', the requirement that someone promising to do something intends to do it, that someone asking for something wants it done, and that someone claiming to know something believes that it is so. Finally, and perhaps most crucially, Searle identified what he called the 'essential condition', the requirement that uttering these particular words does indeed count as the performance of the specified act: thus, saying 'good morrow' or 'hey' must count as the courteous acknowledgement of the hearer by the speaker if the act of greeting is to be successfully brought off. Together, these four conditions specify the axes along which the differences between particular speech acts can be made manifest, or the various levels on which they can differ from each other. But this is not necessarily to say that every speech act must be assessable at each level: for example, in Searle's analysis a greeting lacks propositional content and has no sincerity condition (Searle 1969: 67).

THE THEORY OF SPEECH ACTS: SEARLE'S TAXONOMY

Having formulated the essential structure of the speech act in this avowedly more comprehensive way, Searle went on to explore the classification of speech acts with which Austin had concluded his Harvard lectures. In an essay entitled 'A Taxonomy of Illocutionary Acts' he reconsidered Austin's groupings and once again diagnosed a failure to approach the topic systematically, declaring that 'the first thing to notice about these lists is that they are not classifications of illocutionary acts but of English illocutionary verbs' (Searle 1979: 9). Searle argued that a classification of illocutionary acts cannot proceed by producing loose groupings of the verbs we ordinarily use to characterise what we do in speaking. The demand for a properly or comprehensively systematic theory of speech acts could only be met by reaching deeper levels of classificatory abstraction. Austin's groupings are therefore given over in favour of a new taxonomy that claims to map out the fundamental distinctions, the basic grammar, structuring the field of possible illocutionary acts. Searle now places the emphasis in drawing his distinctions on the crucial matter of illocutionary point or purpose, which he sees as the most elementary difference between kinds of act. And it turns out that this is not as taxing a labour as might be imagined:

There are not, as Wittgenstein (on one possible interpretation) and many others have claimed, an infinite or indefinite number of language games or uses of language. Rather, the illusion of limitless uses of language is engendered by an enormous unclarity about what constitutes the criteria for delimiting one language game or use of language from another. If we adopt illocutionary point as the basic notion on which to classify uses of language, then there are a rather limited number of basic things we do with language: we tell people how things are, we try to get them to do things, we commit ourselves

> to doing things, we express our feelings and attitudes and we bring
> about changes through our utterances.
>
> (Searle 1979: 29)

The first class he calls *assertives*; the second *directives*; the third, *commissives*, survives from Austin's taxonomy; the fourth encompasses what Searle calls *expressives*; and the fifth class is that of *declarations*. Descriptions, reports, statements and the like belong among the assertives; orders and requests are directives; promising and swearing are paradigmatic commissives; and congratulating or apologising are expressives.

The fifth class, though, is slightly tricky for Searle, as his tendency to reconsider its characteristics over the years suggests (Searle 1979: 16, and see Searle and Vanderveken 1985: 56–58, Searle 1989). Declarations are speech acts 'where the state of affairs represented in the proposition expressed is realized or brought into existence by the illocutionary force indicating device [i.e., the element or elements in the speech act that indicate that it is indeed a declaration], cases where, so to speak, "saying makes it so"' (Searle 1979: 16). So, saying 'I resign' in some circumstances just is to resign, while saying 'you're fired' in not unrelated circumstances is to effect the termination of someone else's employment. Attentive readers will recognise that the kind of act here corralled into an illocutionary class apart has the features Austin attributed to the performative utterance in general in his opening lectures. He poses there the question of whether saying can make it so (Austin 1975: 7), and in answering in the affirmative he does not draw any fundamental distinction between declarations of this sort and promises, bets, warnings and orders – precisely the kinds of act separated off in Searle's taxonomy. Furthermore, as we saw in chapter one, the whole thrust of his lectures on speech acts was to break down the initial, heuristic distinction between performative and constative utterances by showing how the judgement of the felicity of performatives generally required some kind of reference to the situation in which they were issued, while constatives in turn were vulnerable to assessment in terms of normative felicity or appropriateness (Austin 1975: 91). And in a later essay Searle too states that all utterances of the type 'I promise . . . ', 'I order . . . ', 'I am asking . . . ', or 'We pledge . . . ', and presumably therefore also such instances as 'I assert . . . ' and 'we are affirming . . . ', are declarations, which might be thought to undermine his own taxonomic distinctions

(Searle 1989: 550). In this framework 'Shut that door!' is just a directive, while 'It's raining' is a simple assertive; 'I order you to shut that door!' would have to be both a directive and a declaration, and similarly 'I tell you it's raining' would be both an assertive and a declaration.

Searle's separation of declarations from other kinds of illocutionary act might therefore seem to be reinstating, at a grammatical level, precisely the kind of categorical distinctions that Austin's investigations strove to undo and that his own later efforts cannot easily sustain. His point, though, in the 'Taxonomy' essay, is that declarations need to be separated off because they alone are completely self-fulfilling: the relation of the illocutionary point of a declaration to its propositional content is unique. 'It is the defining characteristic of this class that the successful performance of one of its members brings about the correspondence between the propositional content and reality, successful performance guarantees that the propositional content corresponds to the world' (Searle 1979: 16–17). Promises, statements or orders don't bring about the situation represented in their propositional content: saying 'I promise to butter the parsnips' butters no parsnips. Declarations are alone in producing the situation they describe, such that if I say you're fired, you're fired; if I say the meeting is adjourned, then the meeting is adjourned. Other speech acts would not appear to change the world of which they speak quite like this: no wonder that Nick Fotion describes declarations as 'linguistic magic' (Fotion 2000: 51). It remains an open question, though, whether this kind of performative sorcery can remain taxonomically bottled up in quite the way that Searle proposes.

THE WORKINGS OF ILLOCUTIONARY ACTS: CONVENTIONS AND COMMITMENTS

As we saw in the previous chapters, *convention* is a key concept in Austin's account of the speech situations that our ways of talking about utterances imply. A speech act involves the invocation of a conventional procedure; if it did not, then a word such as 'promise' could not have the implications it does in fact have. Missing from Austin's account, though, is any sustained exploration of what we mean by 'convention'. Since his death the concept of convention has become more of a topic for debate in the Anglo-American analytic tradition, with discussion often centred around David Lewis's 1969 book, *Convention: A Philosophical*

Study, even though Lewis's detailed and specific definition of a convention serves to exclude a range of practices that might be quite happily accommodated in a looser outline. For Austin, working with just such an outline, describing a speech act as conventional indicates three main characteristics. Firstly, a valid act is one that accords with a shared procedure or way of doing things. Secondly, it is not a natural given: it is an invention, a cultural institution of sorts, and it could probably be otherwise than it actually is. Thirdly, it can be assessed in terms of rightness, appropriateness, or validity: if something is done in accordance with a conventional procedure, then it is done validly. Problems arise, though, from an apparently unavoidable implication of using convention in this looser sense to describe language as a whole. If language is conventional, then does that not imply that there must have been some initial agreement, some founding contract or convening, which instituted or invented it? But such a suggestion, as the American philosopher Willard Quine has put it, is 'not merely unhistorical but unthinkable' (Quine 1969: xi; see also Brodsky Lacour 1992). As we have already seen, Austin's own characterisation of the speech situation as involving rules, norms or procedures, as in some way institutional, is open to such questions, even if he himself does not seek to address them in detail. And as I will show below, they can return to haunt theories of speech acts or performativity.

Thus, for Austin, the exemplary speech situations best suited to the obvious demonstration of his claims for a pragmatic approach to language are those which have a clearly ritual, ceremonial or procedural form: weddings, naming ceremonies, games, legal proceedings of various kinds. For the same reason, four of his six rules for the successful performance of a felicitous act refer to aspects of the conventional procedure that performative verbs imply. But as many of his examples also demonstrate, Austin extends this sense of the conventional nature of illocution to *all* the kinds of speech act that we might perform as speakers of a language: the promise I make to you on the bus tomorrow is as conventional as the vows I took at my wedding. The speech situations that make up the illocutionary dimension of utterance are all conventional in this way. The kind of conventionality that is invoked in formal ritual and ceremonial practices, therefore, is to some extent continuous with that which informs the language we use to conduct our apparently informal everyday interactions. We name ships *this* way, we say, smashing the champagne on the prow; but others do it perfectly well otherwise; we make promises like *this*, but other languages and communities might make them otherwise, or even not make something that we could call a promise at all.

The notion of convention is also important to Austin because it marks a crucial aspect of the difference between illocutionary and perlocutionary components of the speech act. As we saw, the perlocutionary side of the utterance is said by Austin to be ungoverned by any appeal to normative criteria: consequently, '*any*, or almost any, perlocutionary act is liable to be brought off, in sufficiently special circumstances, by the issuing, with or without calculation, of any utterance whatsoever' (Austin 1975: 110). This is not true of the illocutionary side of the speech act, which is why it can be investigated in the way that Austin attempts in his Harvard lectures. It is precisely a matter of invoking procedures or formulae; it requires such an aspect in order to achieve its effects and make its special impact in the world. The investigation of language from this perspective, therefore, calls for utterances to be understood as linguistic events produced or enabled by conventions or rules.

Searle, keen to uncover the deep grammar of the speech act in general and the basis of its varying kinds, inherits from Austin precisely this sense of how illocution works. In his own writings on these topics, though, he once more attempts to sharpen theoretically concepts and distinctions that his predecessor was more reluctant to pursue in this style. Firstly, he argues that our knowledge of the world around us is actually knowledge of two kinds of fact. On the one hand, we are able to make statements about 'brute facts', such as 'this stone is next to that stone' or 'I have a pain' (Searle 1969: 50). These kinds of facts are physical or natural, and their existence does not depend on any conscious human activity. But there is another kind of fact that doesn't appear to be physical in this way, captured in assertions such as 'You owe me five pounds', 'she married him', 'he has been convicted of perjury' or 'the prime minister made a statement to parliament'. These kinds of assertions, says Searle, refer to 'institutional facts':

> They are indeed facts; but their existence, unlike the existence of brute facts, presupposes the existence of certain human institutions. It is only given the institution of marriage that certain forms of behaviour constitute Mr Smith's marrying Miss Jones. . . . At an even simpler level, it is only given the institution of money that I now have a five

dollar bill in my hand. Take away the institution and all I have is a piece of paper with various gray and green markings.

(Searle 1969: 51)

So there are many features of our world that we can only understand if we approach them as institutional facts. We might, Searle argues, be able to observe a game of football as a collection of brute facts, and we might note all kinds of regularities or patterns of behaviour among the people in differently coloured shirts taking part. But however detailed our observations, and however elaborate our analysis of the data we have collected, we could not produce from this standpoint a proper understanding of what was going on. We would not be able to describe what was essential to the event in front of us without invoking institutional facts such as the laws or rules of the game, features as minutely particular as 'offside' or as general as 'team'. Failure to grasp this is a failure to grasp a vital feature of the ontology of our world, the kinds of entities of which it is made: as humans, we are able to use certain brute or natural elements to stand for or carry institutional functions or meanings that are extrinsic to them. This, precisely, is the work of generating conventions, summarised by Searle in the basic formula 'X counts as Y in context C'. So, for example, kicking a ball into a net counts as scoring a goal in the context of a game of football, and emitting a particular string of sounds counts as a sentence meaning 'It is raining' in the context of speaking English. And since we are able to do this, we can go on to make certain institutional facts stand for further institutional facts by invoking the same basic formula on top of a prior invocation. Speech act theory describes just such a process. It shows how uttering a sentence with the propositional content 'It is raining' can count as the performance of various kinds of action in different contexts: making an assertion, asking a question, and so on.

INSTITUTIONS AND CONSTITUTIVE RULES

Institutional facts are therefore the product of our singular ability to invent conventions, to implement the basic 'X counts as Y' rule again and again in ever more elaborate ways. But the sense of 'rule' that Searle relies on here also needs clarification. One can approach rules as instructions that seek to police or control how we behave or how things are done: paradigm instances would be rules such as 'Keep the sabbath day holy' or 'Ties must be worn in the dining room'. Such rules, Searle says, are *regulative*. But the rules characteristic of institutional facts are not really of this kind: they are, instead, *constitutive*:

> Regulative rules regulate antecedently or independently existing forms of behaviour; for example, many rules of etiquette regulate inter-personal relationships which exist independently of the rules. But constitutive rules do not merely regulate, they create or define new forms of behaviour. The rules of football or chess, for example, do not merely regulate playing football or chess, but as it were they create the very possibility of playing such games.
>
> (Searle 1969: 33)

I can, in other words, go to dinner wearing a tie whether or not the rule about ties exists. But I cannot play football independently of its rules, even if I and twenty one others go through something like the same motions. Without its rules, there is no game of football: these rules define how it is done. Institutions, for Searle, are the systematic integration of constitutive rules. Language itself is just such an institution: rules of grammar do not regulate speech activity that we could quite happily conduct beyond them, but instead specify the conventions that are actually constitutive of any such activity. Speech acts, as linguistic acts performed only in accordance with particular pragmatic conventions, are themselves determined by sets of constitutive rules that speech act theory seeks to make explicit. The various kinds of condition that Searle has identified specify the different aspects of the speech act that are governed in this way. What Searle called the 'essential condition' shows this particularly starkly: the claim that saying 'hey' *counts as* courteous recognition presupposes that constitutive rules or determining conventions of the specified kind are in effect.

This assimilation of language to the model of the institution is a revealing if problematic moment in Searle's analysis. On the one hand, it is of a piece with his ambition to characterise the object of his theoretical approach as a system of rules, and to try to spell out that grammatical system in as comprehensive a fashion as possible. Such an entity would therefore have to be understood as precisely the kind of thing that embodies this kind of comprehensive systematicity, just as a discrete institution such as a corporation or a university or a game of chess does. On the other hand, this kind of assimilation ignores all the problems affecting the thinking of language in terms of a calculus or body of rules that Cavell, building on Austin and Wittgenstein, was so keen to highlight. The satisfactions of systematicity can only be bought at the cost of portraying language as an impersonal framework. As we saw in chapter two, this characterisation has political and ethical ramifications. For Austin, speech acts constitute a commitment and a responsibility: words, as he almost put it, are bonds. And this goes for all speech acts, not just obviously commissive utterances such as promises. Following this lead, Searle himself suggests in a recent book that 'a statement simply *is* a commitment to the truth of the expressed proposition' (Searle 2001: 184). This suggestion is continuous with his claim in *Speech Acts* that participating in the procedures of any institution commits us to the observance of its constitutive rules (Searle 1969: 185), and underpins his assertion that 'almost all speech acts have an element of promising about them' (Searle 2001: 181). This is not necessarily a matter of morality for Searle: what is important about it is that it shows one way in which obligations and commitments exist in the world. They are the very texture of the conventionally generated institutions in which we, as linguistic creatures, participate.

THE WORKINGS OF ILLOCUTIONARY ACTS: INTENTIONS AND MEANINGS

There is, however, another side to Searle's theoretical construction of the speech act that threatens to complicate this picture considerably. Together with this account of the role of conventions, Searle also anatomizes the utterance in terms of its meaning. Meaning here, though, has two senses: on the one hand, it is the semantic idea of words or sentences simply having meaning, such that a particular string of phonemes bears with it some idea or concept; on the other, it is what Searle calls 'speaker meaning', what I mean in saying what I say. In order to explicate this he turns to an account of meaning offered by the philosopher of language Paul Grice, progenitor of an account of pragmatics that differs markedly from Austin's. As Searle outlines the notion:

To say that a speaker S meant something by X is to say that S intended the utterance of X to produce some effect in a hearer H by means of the recognition of his intention.

(Searle 1969: 43)

What we have here, then, is an account of meaning as the communication of an intention. The speaker has an intention which informs his or her utterance, and communication occurs when the hearer recognises that intention. Searle qualifies this picture in two ways. Firstly, he insists that this account needs to be confined to the illocutionary aspect of speaking, not the perlocutionary, such that the kinds of intentions recognised must be illocutionary ones such as requesting, or ordering, or vowing. Secondly, this sense of speaker-meaning cannot be disconnected from the meanings conventionally associated with the words one utters:

In the performance of an illocutionary act in the literal utterance of a sentence, the speaker intends to produce a certain effect by means of getting the hearer to recognize his intention to produce that effect; and furthermore, if he is using words literally, he intends this recognition to be achieved in virtue of the fact that the rules for using the expressions he utters associate the expression with the production of that effect.

(Searle 1969: 45)

From this integration of Grice with his own reading of Austin emerges a sense of the speech act as binding together these two aspects such that conventions codify the intentions they also express. It has the obvious merit of capturing a prominent aspect of our common sense way of thinking about how utterance happens.

But rewriting the speech act in this way necessarily involves rearranging an important part of the Austinian furniture, and appears too to run counter to important conditions of our lives in the English language, at least. For a start, this outline places intention at the heart of the utterance as a key constitutive condition. Austin, as we have seen, drew a line between criteria which when unfulfilled result in a 'misfire', and therefore a void speech act, and those which when not met produce infelicity of a different sort. An 'abuse' would not be void: the commitment stands. A wedding that does not accord with the correct procedures will not result in a marriage, but one where I say 'I will' while thinking 'I won't' takes effect with as much illocutionary force as any other. Such insincerity cannot absolve me from the commitments my participation in the conventional procedure has secured.

THE INSINCERE SPEECH ACT

How does Searle cope with such a possibility? His answer is to locate the requirement of an intentional component at two different places in the structure of the speech act. One of these sites is marked by the sincerity condition for acts, so that, for example, a condition of a successful assertion is the speaker's belief that the state of affairs asserted is true, a successful request requires the speaker to want the hearer to do the thing requested, and a successful promise requires the speaker to intend to do the thing promised. But Searle is of course aware that insincere promises are still, crucially, successful. So he revises the rules for promising: the speaker now 'takes responsibility for having the intention rather than stating that he actually has it' (Searle 1969: 62). The function of this for Searle is that it confines the moment of insincerity, the point where there is a breach between intention and performance, to the action promised. Insincere promises, in this analysis, are only empty of the intention to perform what has been promised. The performance of the promise itself, on the other hand, is still necessarily intentional. I may not mean to buy you a drink when I promise to do so, but I still mean to promise. To put it in Searle's terms: the propositional content of an act can be unmeant. This is how lies are possible, too: a statement is made, but the speaker does not believe what he or she is stating. It makes no sense to Searle, however, to say that the illocutionary point of the act can be unmeant, or meant otherwise, in the same way. Whether or not I mean the propositional content, the act is still necessarily intentional. As he says in a later essay, 'I cannot, e.g., promise unintentionally. If I didn't intend it as a promise, then it wasn't a promise' (Searle 1989: 551). The *illocutionary* intention underpinning the act is still therefore one of its primordial or constitutive conditions, such that 'in serious literal speech the sentences are precisely the realizations of the intentions' (Searle 1977: 202). Having thus dealt with a possible problem, the ground is cleared for the baldest of formulations regarding the role of intentions in speech acts in general: 'the author's intention *deter-*

mines which intentional act the author is performing' (Searle 1994: 655; my emphasis). To the extent that it is not a tautology, this means that the character of the acts that we perform in speaking is determined by what we mean to do in speaking.

From this perspective, any attempt to draw Austinian conclusions about the place of intentions in speech acts from the example of the insincere promise, and therefore to make clear how we enter into commitments in speaking, erroneously conflates the two different sites of intentionality, and any such conclusions are therefore predicated on this error. Yet Searle's analysis of the issue is not without its difficulties. For a start, it might be objected that the distinction between these two sites of intentionality, while plausible within the terms of his own theory of speech acts, is a distinction without a real difference. Is it really right to say that what I mean to do, when I promise to do something without meaning to do it, is actually to *promise*? Doesn't the insincerity afflicting the future course of action at the same time change the nature of the speech act performed? From a different standpoint, other, more fundamental problems emerge. One of the consequences of Searle's insistence on a Gricean constitutive intentionality is that speech acts are thereby made logically dependent on our intentions: the speech act is the *manifestation* or *realization* of those intentions, and understanding its workings requires a reference to their determining function. While Searle explicitly dissociates his claims regarding the logical status of intention from the kind of psychological model of speaking that would posit a distinct, private realm of mental or intentional states underlying the outward or public language that bears them, of 'inner pictures animating the visible signs', as he puts it (Searle 1977: 202), his use of terms such as 'realization' or 'expression' to denote the relation between intention and action continually threatens to bring his account into line with such a model.

INTENTIONS AND COMMITMENTS

The claim that the illocutionary point of the standard speech act is a realization of an illocutionary intention is troubling, too, even if the perilous embrace of this psychological model is indeed avoided. Austin's analysis of the false promise was itself offered as a corrective to precisely this model, but it carried very different implications for the relation of intention and action. His point was just that what we *do* in language cannot ordinarily be *essentially* a matter of an intention, illocutionary or otherwise. This is what was marked by the separation of abuses from misfires, of the conditions regarding intentions from those for conventions, and why such conditions must comprehend rather more kinds of possible utterance than the insincere promise. The Cavellian insistence on the necessary implications of our utterances, on what we *must* mean in saying what we do, also comes into play here, since the situation is not unlike that in which the philosopher decides that he is going to abrogate to himself the power to determine what the word 'voluntary' is to mean. For example, whether or not I insulted you in calling you a nerdy swot is not necessarily determined or decided by whether I intended to issue an insult in saying those words, though such illocutionary intentions will in some circumstances be called in evidence should the unhappiness of the situation result in subsequent efforts at excuse or mitigation. An appeal to my intentions, though, will not be the trump card in working out whether in fact I insulted you. What I have *done*, the action performed, is therefore never *primarily* a matter of realizing a determining intention: this is one of the kinds of gap, as Austin suggested, that intervenes between intention and performance in the ordinary language of action. It is therefore a gap that does not need to be interpreted in line with an erroneous or naïve psychology of language, and its invocation need not imply a resort to any such psychology.

Other problems can also be registered. On Searle's account, the commitments that we enter into in speaking are the products of our intentional actions. They are a series of more or less *contractual* obligations that we choose to assume, as Searle himself suggests:

> The notion of an obligation is closely tied to the notion of accepting, acknowledging, recognizing, undertaking, etc., obligations in such a way as to render the notion of an obligation essentially a contractual notion. Suppose a group of people in Australia completely unknown to me sets up a 'rule' whereby I am 'obligated' to pay them $100 a week. Unless I am somehow involved in the original agreement, their claims are unintelligible.
>
> (Searle 1969: 189–90)

In other words, we are only subject to obligations taken on in this conscious, intentional fashion, to the establishment of which we are somehow a consenting party and which we, as conscious agents, must therefore precede. So the model of social interaction that would follow from this is one in which speakers are bound by commitments only to the extent that they entered into them knowingly, intentionally. Indeed, only utterances issued intentionally could even *count* as commitments.

But as we noted in chapter two, the 'shared world' to which our participation in speech situations commits us cannot easily be thought of as assumed in this way, because it is what we learn in learning our language. We cannot therefore invoke a consciousness or intentionality that would precede our utterances logically if not in fact. This is the aspect of the speech situation marked out by the problem of 'tacit consent'. There can be no question of being 'involved in the original agreement' when the agreement we are talking about is a shared world furnished by language itself. The speaking 'I' necessarily finds itself involved in normative situations, in rules, roles and commitments, just in opening its mouth. Searle in fact acknowledges as much in a telling footnote:

> Standing on the deck of some institutions one can tinker with constitutive rules and even throw some other institutions overboard. But could one throw all institutions overboard . . . ? One could not and still engage in those forms of behaviour we consider characteristically human.
>
> (Searle 1969: 186)

The consequences of this position, though, are at odds with his suggestion that only obligations that we mean to take on can bind us, and therefore that a conscious intentionality must constitute the commitments we undertake in our speech acts. Searle's version of the contractual model seems the wrong one for the situation it purports to describe. As we have already seen, there are real difficulties involved in describing language as the result of any kind of 'original agreement'; if these appear in any appeal to the concept of convention they equally afflict the account offered here by Searle.

4

SPEECH ACTS, FICTION AND DECONSTRUCTION
SEARLE, FISH AND DERRIDA

> If you get certain fundamental principles and distinctions about language right, then many of the issues in literary theory that look terribly deep, profound, and mysterious have rather simple and clear solutions. Once you get the foundations right, many (though of course, not all) of the problems are solved.
>
> (Searle 1994: 639)

My previous two chapters have explored how Austin's account of performativity was taken up by a pair of his philosophical inheritors, and sought to draw out the implications of this account as those are registered by, but also continue to affect, those inheritors. Oddly enough, though, the debates around the performative become most heated, and perhaps most dense, when the focus is neither on the 'ordinary language' that was Austin's prime resource and concern nor on Searle's attempt to provide a speech act theoretical analysis of language in general. Instead, the greatest controversy surrounds the utilisation of speech act theory to characterise linguistic phenomena that might appear to be remote from such interests. Most pertinently, a number of theorists quickly saw the potential for adapting the analysis of the performative to provide an understanding of literary and fictional uses of language (see Petrey 1990: 70–111). Austin's own lectures, as we saw in chapter one, had briefly offered a characterisation of literary or fictional speech acts as non-serious; but it was Searle who developed such hints into a full-blown theory of fiction. At the same time, readers of Austin such as the American theorist Stanley Fish and the French philosopher Jacques Derrida saw in the notion of the non-serious performative not an accurate mapping of a new piece of linguistic terrain but a gap or fissure that threatened the coherence and pretensions of the whole enterprise.

SEARLE ON FICTION

Having established to his own satisfaction the systematic or grammatical basis of standard speech acts, and thus apparently realised the promise he saw in Austin's Harvard lectures, Searle then set out to integrate into that system linguistic practices that he considered to be essentially derivative or secondary. So, having analysed the standard case of a literal, serious speech act, he could move on to place the indirect, figurative and non-serious uses of language in relation to this conceptual centre. As he was later to say, 'once one has a general theory of speech acts – a theory which Austin did not live long enough to develop himself – it is one of the relatively simpler problems to analyze the status of parasitic discourse' (Searle 1977: 205). He took fiction to be a prime instance of this kind of parasite, and his account of how it might fit into speech act theory everywhere confirms his sense of its derivative nature. In making Austin's rather sketchy association of fictional utterances with non-serious speech acts the basis for a theory of fiction, Searle seeks to put it on more solid foundations: he intends to provide an account of nothing less than fiction's 'logical status' (Searle 1979: 58–75).

His starting point is a sense of the anomalous nature of fiction from his theoretical perspective. How can it be possible to issue a request or offer an assertion, for example, without it either having the full force of a serious speech act or, if it doesn't, without it thereby being a violation of one of the constitutive conditions for utterances that he has laid out in his general account? If the assertion that 'it is raining' is made but not meant, how is it possible for this to be anything other than an untruth that runs counter to the sincerity condition for assertions? What is it, in other words, that separates fiction from lies? Here he is in fact picking up a very old philosophical issue indeed, traceable to Plato at the latest, and one to which he offers an answer which itself has a lengthy pedigree. Among its canonical expositions is Sir Philip Sidney's celebrated *Defence of Poesy*, in which this paragon of the English Renaissance suggests that fictions and lies are distinct because writers of fiction are not committed to the empirical truth of the claims they make: their narratives or descriptions don't contain lies, because they don't actually make any real assertions about the world. In this, they are paradigmatically contrasted with historians, the validity of whose writings can only properly be assessed by invoking some kind of reference to the world (Sidney [1595] 1966: 52–54).

Searle's preferred contrast is the journalistic report, but the burden of his comparison is substantially similar. Whereas the reportage of a journalist offers an illocutionary act which is serious in being susceptible to assessment in terms of its satisfaction of the standard rules for that act, the fictional utterances of a novelist are 'non-serious' in suspending the customary applicability of those rules. Thus, a *New York Times* journalist's assertion that 'a group of federal, state, and local government officials rejected today President Nixon's idea that the federal government provide the financial aid that would permit local governments to reduce property taxes' invokes, as an assertion, the necessary constitutive conditions for assertions as set out in Searle's taxonomy of illocutionary acts (Searle 1979: 61–62). One of those conditions is that the speaker commits herself, in making the assertion, to the truth of the proposition expressed. If the officials didn't do what the journalist says they did, then she is at best mistaken and maybe even lying. We would have no problem knowing how we might go about determining whether this was indeed the case, and on that basis making just these judgements about her speech act. But the same cannot be said of the fictional speech act. Iris Murdoch's novel *The Red and the Green* begins with an assertive of sorts:

> Ten more glorious days without horses! So thought Second
> Lieutenant Andrew Chase-White recently commissioned in the distin-
> guished regiment of King Edward's Horse, as he pottered contentedly

in a garden on the outskirts of Dublin on a sunny Sunday afternoon in
April 1916.

(Murdoch 1965: 3; quoted in Searle 1979: 61)

But we would not expect the novelist to be committed to the truth of
the proposition here expressed in the same way as the journalist is committed to hers. Murdoch is not affirming that there was an officer of this
name in Dublin in April 1916, nor that he spent any time in the garden
and was looking forward to ten days away from the horses. Since she is
not asserting, she cannot be lying, since lies are a species of infelicitous
assertion. So what is she doing? Where does fiction fit into the system
of speech acts that Searle is seeking to delineate?

PRETENDING

One possible answer is that there is a particular kind of illocutionary
act, of telling a story or writing a novel, in which the writer of fiction is
engaging. Searle is not too keen on this solution, mainly because it
seems to commit us to the implausible notion that fiction involves
the invocation of pragmatic rules that are on the same level as those that
enable us to tell an assertion from a request or a promise. One reason
why this cannot be right is that fictional utterances, as we have seen,
conform in their structure to the rules for all manner of illocutionary
acts, such that we can recognise a fictional assertion as an assertion,
even if of a peculiar sort. Rules of this kind, therefore, cannot serve to
mark the serious off from the non-serious. Searle instead latches on to
the concept of *pretence*. Austin had himself published a lecture on pretending that made a tentative but sophisticated beginning on the
ordinary language exploration of this term (see Austin 1979: 253–71);
his analysis, however, had distinguished between pretending and fiction or play-acting, and insisted that the relation between pretending
and 'really doing' or 'being' was actually quite a complicated one. Searle,
not for the first time, dispenses with such niceties in favour of a more
clear-cut distinction. He acknowledges only two kinds of pretence. Firstly,
there is deception or lying; secondly, there is pretence as 'make-believe':

> To pretend to be or to do something is to engage in a performance
> which is *as if* one were doing or being the thing and is without any

intent to deceive. If I pretend to be Nixon in order to fool the secret service into letting me into the White House, I am pretending in the first sense; if I pretend to be Nixon as part of a game of charades, it is pretending in the second sense.

(Searle 1979: 65)

Fiction is pretending in the second sense: thus, 'Miss Murdoch is engaging in a non-deceptive pseudoperformance which constitutes pretending to recount to us a series of events' (Searle 1979: 65). It is to this extent a kind of frictionless performance of the speech act, a going through the motions: the usual procedures and structures are in play, but they are lifted off from the world. In the 'as if' of fiction, the commitments our utterances ordinarily impose are somehow suspended.

This suspension, though, is not necessarily total. In realist or naturalist fiction in particular a strong degree of friction remains: while it is open to Arthur Conan Doyle to refer to Sherlock Holmes 'as if' such a person actually existed, it is not quite open to him to rearrange the geography of Victorian London in the same way. Should he, in Searle's example, have his protagonist cross the city in a topographically impossible fashion we would not feel unjustified in saying that he had made a mistake. Other cases are less clear cut: is the famous inclusion of a chiming clock in Shakespeare's *Julius Caesar* equally definable as a howler? We might perhaps want instead to suggest that the attempt to define it as such is an imposition of inappropriate conditions on the kind of function Shakespeare's play discharges. What of history plays like *Henry V*, magical realism, or plain old surrealism? But such cases do not necessarily trouble Searle's definition: on the contrary, the fact that we can happily debate the extent of the suspension of ordinary illocutionary commitments in literary works testifies to our understanding of what such a distinction between performance and 'pseudoperformance' involves.

A fundamental question still remains, however: what is it that enables us to tell the forceful from the 'as if', given that the latter must, of necessity, borrow or reproduce the structures and procedures of the former? After all, pretending to cry is only pretending to cry if some or all of the criteria for crying – down turned mouth, red eyes, tears, keening – are fulfilled to an extent. Here Searle appeals to two means of discrimination. The first is the set of what he calls 'horizontal conventions' that enable us to distinguish between assertions about President Nixon that might be open to assessment in terms of accuracy or truth and the kind, for example, that constitute John Adams's opera *Nixon in China*. Here, some sense of fiction as conforming to different rules is necessary; any such rules, though, are not 'on all fours', as Searle puts it, with the basic illocutionary rules that tell, for example, a directive from a commissive, 'but [are] parasitic on them' (Searle 1979: 67). Although Searle does not go on to discuss these conventions, he presumably means the kinds of criterial distinctions between fiction and non-fiction operative in libraries, bookshops and bestseller charts, distinctions that shape the special ways in which novels are distinguished from other kinds of narrative bibliographically, or that allow us to mark out the institutional fact of a theatre from other buildings or spaces and to demarcate an area within it as the special place where all speech acts are to be taken as 'pretended'. Such conventions 'enable the speaker' – the actor on stage, the novelist on the page or at a reading, the singer in performance – 'to use words without undertaking the commitments that are normally required by those meanings' (Searle 1979: 66–67). But what kind of conventions are they? Do they work in the same way as the constitutive rules that Searle outlines in his general theory of speech acts? Or since they do a very different kind of work, should they be understood differently?

PRETENDING AND INTENDING

In accordance with a pattern that should by now be familiar, these conventional criteria for determining the fictional difference are paralleled by a drawing of the distinction in terms of intentionality. Telling the difference here, though, involves the invocation of intentionality not at the level of the sincerity condition that relates to the propositional content of the speech act, nor even simply at the more basic level of the illocutionary point, but according to an implicit and even more basic distinction affecting all utterance:

> Now *pretend* is an intentional verb: that is, it is one of those verbs which contain the concept of intention built into it. One cannot truly be said to have pretended to do something unless one intended to pretend to do it. ... There is no textual property, syntactical or semantic, that will identify a text as a work of fiction. What makes it a work of fiction is, so to speak, the illocutionary stance that the author

takes toward it, and that stance is a matter of the complex illocutionary intentions that the author has when he writes or otherwise com-
poses it.

(Searle 1979: 65–66)

So a fictional promise to mow the lawn is not distinguished from a
proper one by whether or not I do intend to mow the lawn, or even
whether there is a lawn to mow, since a promise that does not fulfil this
sincerity condition might be either fictional or defective; nor does the
distinction emerge at the level of illocutionary intention that distin-
guishes promising to mow the lawn from another illocutionary act with
the same propositional content, since a fictional promise parasitically
copies the structure and procedures of a full promise. Behind all this is a
more fundamental division of the serious from the 'as if', a distinction
between a pretended intention to promise and a valid one. But this division is itself not the bedrock: for Searle, even pretending is irreducibly a
matter of meaning it. Insofar as I pretend to intend, according to Searle
I must intend to do so: the non-seriousness of a fictional speech act,
basic though it is, is therefore contained within a theory of speech acts
that remains committed to an unbreakable tie between illocutionary
force and intentionality. It is always or necessarily possible to determine
the nature of any speech act by reference to the conscious intention that
it realises. A pretended intention is, to this extent, no less fully intentional than a real one. But here, in particular, Searle's account of intentionality comes perilously close to the naïve psychological model that he
elsewhere disavows. Reference to intention is exceptionally pertinent to
the business of telling fictional from non-fictional speech acts, for as
Searle has insisted, they share the same illocutionary structure: this is
precisely why they are appropriately described as *parasitic* on serious
utterances. But if this is so, we might wonder what kind of criteria can
therefore be invoked to distinguish them *at the level of intention*. What
seems to be required is precisely some kind of attitude, disposition or
mental state laid on top of, or lying behind, the grammar of illocution
itself; this, though, is precisely to separate that constitutive grammar
and intentionality in ways that Searle has everywhere resisted. In the
light of such considerations, we might perhaps conclude that furnishing
a speech act theoretical account of fiction is not as simple a problem as
Searle was to claim.

STANLEY FISH: THE RETURN OF THE PERFORMATIVE

Some readers were indeed quick to point out what they saw as fundamental, if not fatal, complications with this attempted clarification of
fiction's logical status. Stanley Fish, a prominent American literary critic
and theorist, homed in on Searle's confident assertion of the distinction
between the serious performance of a speech act and its fictional 'pseudoperformance'. Whereas the philosopher is happy to accept that there
are marginal and difficult cases, instances where the precise determination
of the limits of fiction is a tricky business, he does not think that such
cases trouble the theoretical distinction that he has been able to draw.
Indeed, as I suggested above, the very fact that we can dispute such
cases implies our ready grasp of the distinction at stake. Fish, though,
draws different conclusions. Searle's own acceptance of the ready mixing
of serious and non-serious implies that he cannot appeal to some class of
purely fictional utterances that therefore manage to instantiate his distinction and underwrite its intelligibility. Plenty of apparently non-serious
utterances will contain elements that do seem to make the kind of commitments that we associate with proper speech acts like the journalistic
report, such as Iris Murdoch's assertions about Dublin in 1916, or
Arthur Conan Doyle's claims regarding late Victorian London. And elements of fictional discourse will likewise be found in thoroughly serious
utterances: all those instances where an author or speaker says 'let's
assume . . . ' or 'just imagine . . . '. 'Therefore', Fish says, 'one can make and
hold on to a distinction between fictional discourse and serious discourse
without in any way helping us to answer questions like what is a novel
or a story and how do we tell it from a laundry list?' (Fish 1980: 236–37).

So any classificatory hopes that might be pinned on this distinction
are unlikely to be fulfilled. Nonetheless, of course, its logical validity
remains uncompromised: it still makes logical sense to talk of fiction as
'a kind of discourse that is characterized by the suspension of the rules
to which speech acts are normally held accountable' (Fish 1980: 237).
But Fish now attempts to query Searle's way of characterising what it is
that is temporarily suspended in fictional discourse. Searle's distinction
presupposes that serious utterances involve reference to aspects of their
circumstances that make up the various ways in which their validity
might be assessed, whereas this referential component is suspended in
fictional discourse: fictional utterances only pretend to refer. Thus, a

serious assertion about Napoleon commits the speaker to the truth of what is asserted about Napoleon, whereas a pretended assertion about a cavalry officer, a detective, or even about 'Napoleon', a fictional character, involves no such commitment. Fish, though, reads this distinction as implicitly separating out a discourse that is responsible to 'facts' or the real world, on the one hand, from one that is cut free of such responsibilities. His point in saying this is to argue that the distinction between the serious and the non-serious cannot be one between a discourse that refers out beyond itself to something real and one that does not, since the real itself, precisely that which is to be allowed to count as real, is determined conventionally: all serious speech acts themselves follow these properly and thoroughly conventional procedures, and such conventional procedures and the distinctions they underpin are the product of human inventiveness or creativity.

For Fish, Searle's separation of fiction as pretence from ordinary or non-pretended utterance conceals a telling implication of his own arguments about the conventional basis of all the ways in which we carry on our real and substantial business in the ordinary world. If such commitments are conventional, then they are to some degree made up, and we are, in this strictly limited if not actually improper sense, pretending all the time. In talking about fictional characters, Searle says, we engage in 'shared pretense' (Searle 1979: 71). Fish argues, though, that the conclusion one should draw from the elaboration of speech act theory is that

> 'shared pretense' is what enables us to talk about anything at all. When we communicate, it is because we are parties to a set of discourse agreements which are in effect decisions as to what can be stipulated as a fact. It is these decisions and the agreement to abide by them, rather than the availability of substance, that make it possible for us to refer, whether we are novelists or reporters for the *New York Times*. One might object that this has the consequence of making all discourse fictional; but it would be just as accurate to say that it makes all discourse serious, and it would be better still to say that it puts all discourse on a par.
>
> (Fish 1980: 242–43)

So in the end it is Searle's characterisation of fiction as pretence, and the possible implication one might draw from this that ordinary utterance is somehow more fundamentally answerable to the real world, that is Fish's target. He reads this characterisation as inscribing in speech act theory a distinction that actually runs counter to its best insights into the nature of the web of 'institutional facts' that we, as linguistic creatures, actually inhabit.

To read Searle in this way is certainly to read him against the grain. Yet Fish was not alone in his unease about the characterisation of non-serious speech acts, as we shall see, and insofar as Searle's notion of pretence built on Austin's own asides about fiction, then such unease could also be registered in relation to the formulations of the initial Harvard lectures. In a lengthy headnote prefacing the article in which he advances his critique of Searle, Fish does indeed apply his point about fiction to the very initial formulations with which Austin began. Here, Fish characterises the basic distinction between performatives and constatives in a revealing fashion:

> Constative language is language that is, or strives to be, accountable to the real or objective world. It is to constatives – to acts of referring, describing, and stating – that one puts the question 'Is it true or false?' in which true and false are understood to be *absolute* judgments, made independently of any particular set of circumstances. Performative language, on the other hand, is circumstantial through and through. The success of a performative depends on certain things being the case when it is uttered; performatives are therefore appropriate or inappropriate in relation to a reality that underlies all conditions.
>
> (Fish 1980: 198)

That reality, though, is the reality of human discourse agreements, the sets of institutions that enable us to have a meaningful world in the first place. So when the distinction between constative and performative is shown to be unsustainable, what goes with it is precisely this notion of a reference to a world that is not somehow dependent on those agreements. In Fish's argument, but not in Searle's or Austin's, another casualty of this failed distinction is an apparently homologous one between fictional and serious utterances:

> All facts are discourse specific (since no fact is available apart from some dimension of assessment or other) and ... therefore no one can claim for any language a special relationship to the facts as they

'simply are,' unmediated by social or conventional assumptions. This, however, is precisely the claim traditionally made for 'serious' or 'real-world' language as opposed to literary language, and it is this distinction that I challenge.

(Fish 1980: 199)

In Fish's account, then, fictional or literary language is to serious utterance precisely as the performative is to the constative in Austin's lectures: the same kind of apparently special case whose seemingly peculiar features turn out to be characteristic of the general situation. Yet this ranging of the performative, literary or fictional on one side against the constative, the referential, or the serious on the other has some profound and distorting implications. Firstly, the frictionless inventiveness of literary creativity comes to resemble the performative capacity of 'saying' to 'make it so', the linguistic magic that Austin only provisionally contrasted with the statement or assertion, and that Searle confined to the peculiarly world-creating powers of declarations. Secondly, ordinary language, insofar as it can here be contrasted with fiction or the performative, is thereby strangely aligned with the constative or descriptive, when the whole point of Austin's resort to the ordinary was to hold the pragmatics of the speech act up against a logical positivist model of language as essentially constative. In Fish's hands, the whole project of speech act theory has been reoriented, and thus rearranged, so that it begins to speak against itself from the opening furnished by its characterisation of fiction.

DERRIDA READS AUSTIN

The attention paid by Fish to this aspect of Searle's thinking, along with his sense that the distinction between serious and fictional speech acts might be ultimately untenable, echoes the reading of Austin's Harvard lectures pursued by the profoundly influential philosopher Jacques Derrida. Derrida's reading of Austin was his closest engagement with modern Anglo-American philosophy, a very different approach to the discipline from his own; it is perhaps not surprising, therefore, that it should also have been the trigger for one of the most acrimonious disputes of his long career. Derrida's initial essay, entitled 'Signature Event Context' was delivered as a lecture in Montreal in 1971, and published in an English translation in 1977. This essay elicited a forceful response from John Searle (Searle 1977), which almost immediately triggered a detailed, caustic reply by Derrida, 'Limited Inc a b c . . . ' (see Derrida 1988: vii–viii). Further pot-shots were taken by Searle in subsequent essays (Searle 1983, 1994), and partisans on both sides weighed in with gusto, while others wondered whether the heated exchanges ever shed much light on the questions and claims at issue (Dasenbrock 1989; Petrey 1990: 131–46; Bearn 1995; Gorman 1999). Either way, the context of his dispute with Searle has loomed large for those who have sought to draw out the implications of Derrida's resort to Austin. It is not my intention here, though, to offer what would probably be a repetitive narrative of points missed and arguments reiterated. Instead, I want to make as clear as possible not only the claims made by Derrida in his reading of Austin, but also the justifications he offers for those claims and their implications for both the theory of performativity and the broader enterprise of philosophy itself.

THE STATUS OF FICTION: SERIOUSNESS AND CITATIONALITY

The starting point for Derrida's engagement is Austin's brief description of fictional utterances, precisely the description that Searle was later to take over as the basis for his account of fiction's 'logical status':

> A performative utterance will, for example, be *in a peculiar way* hollow or void if said by an actor on the stage, or if introduced in a poem, or spoken in soliloquy. This applies in any and every utterance – a sea-change in special circumstances. Language in such circumstances is used not seriously, but in ways *parasitic* upon its normal use – ways which fall utter the doctrine of the *etiolations* of language.
>
> (Austin 1975: 22)

What gives Derrida his cue here is the kind of language that Austin uses to mark the separate status of fictional utterances as non-serious. If such utterances are hollow or void, then they are to be contrasted with the full or substantial utterances of ordinary language; that they should be characterised as hollow seems to make of them mere shells, shadows, or insubstantial images of the utterance proper. In the same way, an etiolation is a pale instance of something that in its proper form is much more vivid, a weakened rendering of an original strength. The most interesting set of connotations, though, comes from the definition of fictional utterances as *parasitic* on normal or ordinary uses: not only does such a term suggest that fictional performatives merely copy, or derive from, proper performatives; there is also an unavoidable if attenuated invocation of a moral context. Parasites are unworthy, living off the strength and life of the hosts they infect or infest. Derrida also remarks on the fact that Austin appears to exclude the consideration of such parasites from his account of the workings of the performative. Such a move, Derrida suggests, implies a belief that one can first of all establish what constitutes a normal speech act and then, like Searle, proceed to add the analysis of fiction to this primary theory.

So on this reading Austin's account posits a distinction between original, substantial, normal or valid performatives and secondary, hollow, abnormal ones. The parasitic nature of these latter is clearly seen in the fact that they are quotations or citations of original performatives, mimicking the form but lacking the illocutionary force or substance of that which they cite. For Derrida, though, this distinction is undermined by Austin's equally strong insistence that proper performatives are conventional in nature, 'iterable' or repeatable, and therefore in order to succeed must involve what amounts to the recitation of an already written script:

> Isn't it true that what Austin excludes as anomaly, exception, 'non-serious', *citation* (on stage, in a poem, or a soliloquy) is the determined modification of a general citationality . . . without which there would not even be a 'successful' performative? . . . Could a performative utterance succeed if its formulation did not repeat a 'coded' or iterable utterance, or in other words, if the formula I pronounce in order to open a meeting, launch a ship or a marriage were not identifiable as *conforming* with an iterable model, if it were not then identifiable in some way as a 'citation'?
>
> (Derrida 1988: 17, 18)

If valid or original speech acts themselves involve an essential element of citation, this citationality cannot be marked off as that which invalidates fictional performatives as non-serious. Insofar as they are conventional in nature, repetitions of an established procedure or formula, even felicitous performatives are characterised by the hollowness or deriva-tiveness that Austin seeks to ascribe only to abnormal performatives, and that allows him to describe them precisely as parasitic. In which case, Austin's separation of the serious from the non-serious can only be a *dogmatic* or arbitrary move with no rational basis in the logic to which it nonetheless seems to appeal. Derrida's deconstructive intervention seeks to reveal this hidden dogmatism. At the same time, it shows how the implicit prioritising of the serious over the non-serious, of the sub-stantial over the hollow or of the host over the parasite, is undermined by teasing out the logic of Austin's own arguments, and how that logic therefore works against the implicit value judgements it has been held to underpin. If successful performatives are necessarily citations of a sort, then the derivative is already at work in the original, and the etio-lating parasite actually characterises or constitutes the vigorous host. By the same token, any attempt to determine the nature of the substantial or valid act first, and only secondarily to consider fictional or hollow ones, is doomed to be equally dogmatic: even if it were only to be made provisionally, it would precisely serve to prejudge the issue in a way that Derrida's deconstruction shows to be rationally unjustified.

COMMUNICATION AND THE MARK

On this evidence, a deconstructive approach leaves the characterisation of fiction's logical status within an Austinian account of the performa-tive in some difficulty, with obvious consequences for Searle's attempt to build on these foundations. Though this appears formally similar to Fish's argument, the fact that it is based not on fiction's status as pre-tended reference but on a consideration of it as 'citation' indicates important differences in the approach taken. Most significantly, it ensures that for Derrida the focus remains on the felicity or validity, the illocutionary force, of the performative or speech act. Derrida's decon-struction of this distinction between the infelicities of fiction and the validity of the serious utterance occurs within a more fundamental unsettling of speech act assumptions that in the end presents an influen-tially different way of making sense of linguistic performativity. For a start, his approach to Austin in 'Signature Event Context' begins not with fiction, but with an excursus on assumptions regarding the nature of communication that he identifies as the implicit underpinnings of speech act theories. What, Derrida asks, do we mean by communication? The most obvious model is that of a meaning, an idea or set of ideas, carried across from one person to another. Certainly, Austin's model of the 'speech situation' might seem to require something like communication of this kind to be going on, insofar as the idea of a speech situation must require the gathering of speaker and hearer around a communicated meaning; Searle's Gricean notion of a 'speaker meaning', or an intention communicated to a hearer, is more explicitly indebted to such a view, since a hearer's failure to grasp the speaker's illocutionary intention amounts to the failure of the speech act properly to take place.

Derrida's investigation involves asking an apparently naïve question: what makes communication possible? This is not just an empirical issue: it is not primarily a matter of asking what makes any group of communicative occasions possible. Instead, Derrida is asking what makes communication in general, in principle, possible. His answer tracks those given by various philosophical predecessors in invoking a model of language as the bearer of sense or meaning, but he gives it a distinctive twist by noting how such a model presupposes an idea of meaning determined as a kind of presence: the meaning is a unified and distinct entity, a self-sufficient idea or intention; it is present to the mind of its speaker, and by the good offices of language it can also become present to the mind of a hearer too. Communication would thus be intersubjective: what is present to my mind is made present to yours, too. When I have successfully managed to convey to you thoughts, dispositions, feelings that are immediately present to me, communication has taken place. Language is thus identified as the primary means of extending meaning as presence in this way. Speech transports mental contents if you or another recipient are in earshot; in other circumstances, writing is able to stand in for speech. So writing often takes the place of speech, and allows us as interlocutors to overcome the perhaps unavoidable absence from each other that might otherwise make communication impossible. You can get my meaning by reading this book, just as well as if I were talking directly to you: the writing here serves to transport my idea across the distance in time and space that separates us. Derrida points out, though, how writing is both credited with this capacity to extend the reach of presence by overcoming the impediments that distance or absence afflicts on communication and also seen as inferior, as a less reliable vehicle than speech. Writing is more liable than speech to confound communication: its capacity to extend presence is coupled with an increased danger of producing a breakdown in communication, of breaching the presence of my meaning to you that communication should afford.

ITERABILITY

So, putting it somewhat crudely, the picture of communication that Derrida paints depicts discrete units of meaning travelling out into the world via speech and writing, and running a greater risk of failing to get through the further out they have to go. If Derrida finds this model dubious, it is because it portrays this breach in presence, this absence, as a contingent risk that communication runs only as it takes place: it is not something that belongs to it *in principle*, as a necessary element in its structure. The analysis he proposes seeks to show, on the contrary, how communication is not even thinkable without the resort to a certain notion of absence or breach. In order to do this, he emphasises what he calls the *iterability* of the linguistic elements necessary for the communication of meaning, whether they be spoken or written. The notion of iterability points to a necessary feature of linguistic elements as such, a quality they must have if they are indeed to be considered linguistic. Specifically, it refers to the repeatability of which linguistic units must be capable: a sign or a mark that was not repeatable would not be a sign or a mark, and could not be an element in a language or a code. This goes for all marks, for marks as such, even if one could be found that had actually occurred only once: when it was uttered or written, as a mark it was constituted by the fact that it was repeatable, by its iterability.

Yet if marks are necessarily iterable in this fashion, certain consequences follow. Firstly, the mark must be capable of functioning in what Derrida calls the 'radical absence' of any particular party to communication (Derrida 1988: 8). This absence is radical because it is not just a matter of the distance between parties, but of their death or disappearance; or rather, it is radical because for the mark to be a mark it must be capable of functioning in supreme indifference to the existence or otherwise of any particular sender or receiver. Even if there were a language known only to two people, one that they had invented and used only to convey their innermost thoughts to each other, insofar as it was a *language* it would have to be iterable, to be essentially capable of working in the absolute absence of either or both of them. So this 'rupture in presence' is not a threat to the working of linguistic communication: on the contrary, such a rupture, a breaking off from sender or receiver, is necessary for language to work as such (Derrida 1988: 8).

Secondly, the very iterability that allows a mark to be repeated – that allows one letter 'a' to be a repetition of another letter 'a', for example – also introduces an irreducible difference into the structure of the mark. Each letter 'a' might well be recognisable as the same as any *other* letter 'a', but this sameness also implies their difference from each other. It is for this reason that we can say that 'a' and 'A' are the same as each other even while their difference cannot be ignored; but this is not an orthographic matter, since even two marks that look identical must be understood as different from each other simply because there are two of them. If a mark is iterable, it must be capable of occurring again, elsewhere, some other time: iterability allows the sameness of the mark only on the condition of this structural, internal difference. A mark, in other words, is therefore never quite identical with itself, never quite unified or entire of itself. This difference has to be understood as original, as constitutive of the mark, and operative in any mark that we might want to think of as the original one, as the first of its kind. Even the first mark, insofar as it is a mark, is internally riven in this way: even the first letter 'a', could we imagine such a thing, could only be identified as such because it already looked like others of its kind. To this extent, no mark is ever a thing, or an entity, or a discrete unit of meaning. It is what it is only by virtue of this internal difference from itself.

Thirdly, insofar as a mark is iterable, it cannot be said to belong either ultimately or originally in any particular context. If it is essentially repeatable, it can be extracted from any set of linguistic or social circumstances and grafted into another, remaining in some way the same as it is repeated. It can, in other words, be redeployed, quoted, or cited, in principle *ad infinitum*. And this capability also ensures that its use in any particular context carries the trace of the other contexts in which it features: the examples of quoting and citing reveal this particularly starkly. No mark, then, can finally be traced back to a resting place in an original and unified context. But as Derrida puts it, 'this does not imply that the mark is valid outside of a context, but on the contrary

that there are only contexts without any center or absolute anchorage'
(Derrida 1988: 12).

This notion of iterability, then, allows Derrida to query the picture
of communication as involving the presence of a unified meaning to a
speaker and a hearer. It permits him to argue that interruptions to presence such as rupture, breach, or difference are not an external limit to
presence or communication but, in a sense that is not always easy to
grasp, already on their inside. And to the extent that the speech act is
understood as a scene of communication, of the transmission of a meaning,
then the same consequences apply. Derrida's emphasis on the structural
openness of context would affect any sense of a context as an enclosed
'speech situation' with its limits built into it. Iterability also implies
that any sense of a performative as identical with, or as the fulfilment of,
an intention becomes problematic, precisely because the iterability of
any utterance means that it works on the basis of a radical absence from
its utterer, even if a hearer receives the utterance straight from the
horse's mouth, as it were. This is the condition of such communication:
this is why, for instance, I can write a will, and my instructions can be
read and followed even after I am dead; but this capability can only be
bought at the cost of a breach in the self-presence of my meaning that
even affects the occasion of my writing or speaking the words.

The idea that a standard speech act might be the realisation or presentation of a complete, unitary meaning or intention is therefore put in
question by this focus on the linguistic structure of such an act: as language it is not in principle capable of the intentional fullness, the self-
presence, that such notions as 'speaker meaning' would seem to imply.
So here we can see the distinctive basis for Derrida's deconstruction of
Austin's classification of the non-serious or fictional performative. If all
speech acts, as linguistic acts, are constituted on the basis of a fundamental iterability, then it cannot make sense to hive off a separate class
of hollow or 'unmeant' performatives on the grounds that Austin, and
Searle after him, appear to adduce. One cannot simply draw the boundary between serious and non-serious performatives on the grounds that
the former are fully meaningful or intentional, while others are mere
citations at a distance of such meanings, empty copies cut off from that
fullness. The citationality that characterises a quoted or parasitic utterance is itself a more local name for the general iterability that characterises all language, and therefore all speech acts or performatives.

THE NECESSITY OF ITERABILITY

In order to grasp the broader implications of Derrida's intervention, we need to be clear about the particular status of his claims as I have outlined them here. Why is it, for example, that a suggestion that marks are repeatable should be held to imply that my utterance, here, now, can't be the fulfilment and the embodiment of an intention? How can the fact that some utterances are citations of prior utterances entail any consequences for a theory of how proper, standard speech acts work, or for a sense of how they work in theory? Why should the plain fact that some speech acts are infelicitous, or that communication sometimes breaks down, have any consequences for the general account of performative language as that is laid out by Austin or Searle? After all, stuff happens: the fact that things don't always work out according to the ideal shouldn't necessarily mean that we need to amend the standard model proposed by the theory.

Such a view would be of a piece with the notion of communication as the transmission of units of meaning, where the transmission of such meaning is threatened only empirically, by accidents in the empirical world which can always befall it but which have no bearing on the structure or constitution of the communication they interrupt. Thus, to use an example close to one of Derrida's, I might write you a letter expressing my innermost thoughts, and it might get lost in the sorting office, and never arrive. Or else I might be about to give you a piece of my mind, and then a car alarm goes off nearby, and you can't hear a word I say. Had the letter not been lost, or had the car alarm not gone off, then communication would have taken place in precisely the way the theory requires, with the transmission of a unit of meaning. So the fact that some performatives are infelicitous in various ways says nothing about the potential validity or felicity of others. How, then, can pointing to such infelicities in any way imperil the theory? As Derrida himself puts it, imagining just this objection:

> You cannot deny that there are also performatives that succeed, and one has to account for them: meetings are called to order . . . ; people say: 'I pose a question'; they bet, challenge, christen ships, and sometimes even marry. It would seem that such events have occurred. And

even if only one had taken place only once, we would still be obliged
to account for it.

(Derrida 1988: 17)

Searle, precisely in line with this objection, assumes that the fact that
there are dubious, parasitic or infelicitous speech acts is completely
irrelevant to the business of formalising or systematising the speech act
in general. So, in setting out his understanding of the promise in *Speech
Acts*, he readily acknowledges that he is 'going to deal with a simple and
idealized case', and that his 'analysis will be directed at the center of the
concept of promising. I am ignoring marginal, fringe and partially
defective promises' (Searle 1969: 55–56). For the same reason, as we
have seen, he was happy to build an account of the logical status of fiction as an addendum to a general theory of standardly valid speech acts.
If promises have sometimes been made, and it seems that they have,
then why not analyse the basic structure of such valid promises first,
and worry about the various kinds of invalidity that might afflict other
attempted promises later?

Derrida's target here, though, is precisely this sense of how the ideal
or proper structure of the standard speech act relates to the flaws,
breakdowns, ruptures and absences to which it is liable. He notes with
interest Austin's own acknowledgement that 'as utterances, our performatives are . . . heir to certain other kinds of ill which infect *all* utterances'
(Austin 1975: 21), the 'kinds of ill' in question here being the capacity
to be cited, quoted, or otherwise used 'non-seriously'. Other claims Austin
makes about failed or non-standard performatives share this general
reference, as I noted in chapter one: they too are claims about vulnerabili-
ties shared by *all* speech acts, by speech acts *in general*. Firstly we find
him asserting that 'infelicity is an ill to which *all* acts are heir which
have the general character of ritual or ceremonial, all *conventional*
acts' (Austin 1975: 18–19); shortly afterwards, he suggests that, considered as *actions*, performatives are 'subject to certain whole dimensions of
unsatisfactoriness to which all actions are subject', and that certain infelicities can be said to apply to 'actions in general' (Austin 1975: 21). Later
still, in a brief but telling prefiguration of Derrida's reading, he
describes speech acts as 'essentially mimicable, reproducible' (Austin
1975: 96). So, despite saying that he is excluding such infelicities from
consideration, he seems to accept that they belong to the speech act as

such. If that is the case, then any general account of linguistic performativity, any account that claims to be able to tell us not what a particular selection of empirical performatives are like but how performatives in general *must be*, therefore has to account for the possibility of these infelicities too. If speech acts can be infelicitous, and if such problems apply as possibilities to them all, then a full account of the performative must explain this general possibility.

When Austin recognises that the risk of infelicity is one to which all speech acts are exposed by virtue of their constitution, Derrida asks, how does he then understand this kind of general peril?

> Does the quality of risk admitted by Austin surround language like a kind of *ditch* or external place of perdition which speech ... can escape by remaining 'at home', by and in itself, in the shelter of its essence or *telos*? Or, on the contrary, is this risk rather its internal and positive condition of possibility? Is that outside its inside, the very force and law of its emergence?
>
> (Derrida 1988: 17)

The recognition that speech acts, as conventional procedures and as forms of action, are *necessarily* exposed to certain ills points away from the former option and towards the latter. In other words, Derrida wants to draw out the consequences of Austin's recognition of an *essential* risk through his focus on the iterability that characterises all linguistic structures. His account of iterability therefore points towards a possibility of infelicity that lies at the heart of the structure of the performative, that makes it what it is, rather than prowling around outside it as a merely external threat that has no necessary bearing on that structure. By insisting on iterability as the condition of the possibility of the speech act *per se*, as something presupposed by Austin's account of the general structure of the performative, Derrida is locating the possibility of infelicity – of rupture, breach, 'hollowness' – within that general structure. The ruptures or breaches that iterability denotes, that is to say, are not things that might befall a particular and unfortunate performative while leaving standard, valid performatives untouched: they are an essential element in *how all performatives must happen*, constitutive of their felicitous taking place as much as of any potential infelicity.

DERRIDA'S TRANSCENDENTAL ARGUMENTS

Derrida's argument here is operating at the level of *necessary conditions*. Austin's own sense of the pragmatic dimension, in Cavell's reading, gains its distinctive philosophical purchase from the fact that it claims to reveal such conditions: the propositions of ordinary language philosophy articulate the necessities inhabiting language in use, rather than merely describing the regularities of any particular speech situation in the manner of an empirical science. The necessity that Derrida's reading of Austin draws out of its topic is of a related, but not quite identical character. Derrida is concerned to explore the conditions for the possibility of the speech act, those features that any theory of the performative must presuppose. His argument has therefore been described as having a *transcendental* character, following the example of the eighteenth century German philosopher Immanuel Kant, whose 'transcendental idealism' sought to show how human experience can only be possible on the basis of certain conditions that can be known *a priori* and therefore articulated philosophically. Searle's pursuit of a general theory of speech acts, as shown in his claim to have set out an exhaustive taxonomy of illocutionary acts, for example, reveals something of the same ambition to articulate the necessities of language use. Yet he is much more sanguine about, and far less interested in, marginal, infelicitous or non-standard speech acts than Austin, and in his dispute with Derrida he persistently refuses the idea that the issue can have any bearing on the structure of the felicitous speech act in general (see Searle 1977; 1994). His confidence is based, though, on an unexamined resort to precisely the distinction between essence and accident, between what something is in itself and what might or might not affect it from the outside, that Derrida's deconstruction places under such strain. Far more clearly than Austin, perhaps because he is seeking to set out a general theory of language when his predecessor is not, Searle depends in his analysis on the dogmatic separation of centre from margins, standard from deviant, essence from accident.

Yet if Derrida's analysis is to some degree a transcendental one, it also generates problems for exactly this kind of philosophical accounting. As we have seen, he shows how the ruptures or breaches of which he speaks are essential to the functioning of the standard speech act, in that one can say of iterability that it is necessarily presupposed by the thinking even of the successful performative. It is an *a priori* or transcendental condition of the possibility of any speech act in general. Yet at the same time, it cannot simply be a condition of the *possibility* of the valid speech act since it compromises in advance the structural integrity or unity claimed for it by Searle's 'idealization', and therefore serves to disrupt that very possibility. So iterability, by a strange and difficult logic, is both the condition of the possibility of performative felicity *and* the condition of its strict impossibility. What Searle would exclude as 'deviant, marginal or parasitic' turns out to be necessarily implicated in the validity of what he characterises as the 'standard' speech act. It enables it to take place, but only on the condition that it cannot be structurally distinguished from the invalid. As Derrida suggests:

> A standard act depends as much upon the possibility of being repeated, and thus potentially of being mimed, feigned, cited, played, simulated, parasited, etc., as the latter possibility depends upon the possibility said to be opposed to it. And both of them 'depend' upon the structure of iterability which, once again, undermines the simplicity of the oppositions and alternative distinctions. It blurs the simplicity of the line dividing inside from outside, undermines the order of succession or of dependence among the terms.
>
> (Derrida 1988: 91–92)

As a rather peculiar kind of transcendental condition, arrived at through the *a priori* thinking of the speech act in general but not letting such thinking come to rest in its conclusions, iterability 'limits what it makes possible, while rendering its rigor and purity impossible'. It is, he suggests, 'something like a law of undecidable contamination' (Derrida 1988: 59), an obligation to think the *necessary* contamination of presence with absence, of the serious with the feigned, of essence with accident, and as difficult to apprehend as these kinds of formulation would suggest. Which is not to say that this is where thinking grinds to a halt, or that all distinctions merge into some kind of hapless indeterminacy. Derrida is keen to avoid any suggestion of such a nihilistic outcome:

> By no means do I draw the conclusion that there is . . . no performative effect, no effect of ordinary language, no effect of presence or of discursive event (speech act). It is simply that those effects do not exclude what is generally opposed to them, term by term; on the contrary,

they presuppose it, in an asymmetrical way, as the general space of their possibility.

(Derrida 1988: 19)

In other words, if the fundamental distinctions on which the theory of speech acts would appear to depend have been shown to undermine each other, then if we now wish to speak of differences between valid and invalid speech acts, and if we now wish to explore in this way the general or necessary structure of the performative, we can no longer do so on the bases proposed by speech act theory. This is precisely the challenge taken up by Derrida in subsequent work, and it is one of the most important aspects of his engagement with the concept of performativity that he finds new and unexpected resonances of the term in doing so.

AUSTIN AND THE NON-SERIOUS PERFORMATIVE

Before going on to explore the ramifications and underpinnings of Derrida's engagement with Austin, it is worth pausing to ask just how telling his deconstruction of the latter's account of the difference between serious and non-serious speech acts actually is. At its most basic and widely understood, Derrida's case involves the claim that Austin's distinction between valid and invalid speech acts is predicated on a distinction between fully meant and merely citational utterances that the account of the 'proper' speech act does not uphold. Austin has given a criterion for the difference which cannot be logically sustained, and can therefore only be dogmatically asserted. The distinction must be understood as a more contingent, pragmatic or political matter, rather than a fundamental difference in kind between substantial original and mere copy. Austin's theoretical distinctions would therefore function as an attempt to trump contingency or politics with the mobilisation of a dissimulated metaphysics of seriousness. Against this, Derrida suggests that 'rather than oppose citation or iteration to the noniteration of an event, one ought to construct a differential typology of forms of iteration' (Derrida 1988: 18). Were it at all feasible, this would permit the exploration of the fact that some citations matter in a different way from others without conniving at the naturalisation of the difference.

The difficulty, though, is that Austin does not picture the difference between serious and citational utterances in this way. He does suggest that 'non-serious' utterances are in some way 'parasitic' on 'serious' ones, and that when someone is joking, writing a poem or reciting a soliloquy the kinds of commitment that might follow in other circumstances do not apply. But such a claim need not entail the assertion that such activities are *nothing other than* pale imitations of our ordinary speech acts. A style of philosophy like Austin's, furthermore, riddled as it is with jokes, irony, puns, citations and allusions, could hardly be expected to assume that seriousness and playfulness are simply opposed to each other in such a fashion (for this aspect of Austin's writing, see especially Felman 2002 and Ricks 1996). Neither does Austin in fact suggest that the difference between serious and non-serious utterances is that the former are filled out with a constitutive intention. As we saw in chapter one, intention is not the dominant criterion of seriousness for Austin, even if reference to intention is a pragmatic implication of such performative verbs as asserting, promising and ordering. It is therefore not an infallible or fundamental criterion of felicity, since felicity and seriousness coincide: speech acts that fail to live up to this implication can still be invested with illocutionary force. Derrida's suggestion, therefore, that for Austin 'the conscious presence of the intention of the speaking subject in the totality of his speech act' remains the main condition for the proper performative is misleading at the very least (Derrida 1988: 14; see also Petrey 1990: 138). Neither the 'sea-change in special circumstances' that Austin invoked when speaking of the non-serious, nor other ways of drawing the distinction between the felicitous and infelicitous speech act, can be translated into a claim that there is an ontological difference between acts in which an intention is manifested and those that are empty citations.

Derrida is in fact too quick to assume that Austin is engaged in establishing securely transcendental constitutive conditions for the speech act, an assumption that has misled a number of readers over the years with occasionally disastrous consequences (see, especially, Miller 2001: 6–62). This, though, is to ignore the distinctive character of the necessities that Austin's philosophical practice is in fact seeking to draw out of language as action, and in particular to disregard the project of ordinary language philosophy within which Austin's Harvard lectures were formulated. To say that asserting or promising or requesting necessarily implies or commits us to believing or intending or wanting is to draw attention to the ways in which our language remarks upon the pragmatic implications of saying something. It is not to offer a theory, either cut free from or underpinning 'ordinary language', of the transcendental conditions of the possibility of speaking as such. Austin's brief remarks on 'seriousness' are therefore not an attempt to establish what must be the case, what conditions must obtain, if there is to be any proper speech act; they are, at most, a somewhat perfunctory nod towards a distinction that ordinary language makes possible, and which an interest in the normativity of language might lead someone like Austin to wonder at: how is it, why is it, that we can designate some threats, descriptions, orders and so on as ones that count, ones that institute a commitment, while others that are recognisably of the same kind are not subject to, or do not issue in, the same demands?

This also means that the 'ordinary' in Austin's sense cannot on these grounds be characterised as a source of philosophical certainty (see Cavell 1994: 59–127). To some extent, Derrida repeats the mistake attributed to Stanley Fish earlier in this chapter: focusing on Austin's characterisation of the non-serious and its opposition to the ordinary, Derrida too neglects the ways in which his sense of the latter reflects critically on philosophy's traditional quest for some kind of properly solid foundation underlying the matrix of our linguistic lives, what Cavell calls its 'chronic *false* seriousness' (Cavell 1994: 125). In this context, it is certainly interesting to note that Austin does not just use the term 'parasite' to characterise fictional or citational utterances. In the discussion following a lecture he gave on the subject of performative utterances, he also described the experience of promising oneself something, of communicating with oneself, as 'parasitic' on the business of issuing public speech acts (Austin 1963: 39). For Austin, in other words, if the ordinary and ordinary language are in some sense the focus for philosophy, such a focus does not necessarily imply the primacy of self-consciousness, or self-presence, in the way that Derrida's analysis suggests. On the contrary, the apparent self-presence of talking to oneself or hearing oneself speak would itself be parasitic on, derivative of, the exigencies of talking to others. What Derrida lacks in his reading of Austin at this point, in other words, is sufficient sense that seriousness, or ordinary language, might not simply be substitute terms for the kind of indubitably solid foundations that philosophy has often hoped to establish.

5

PERFORMATIVITY, ITERABILITY AND POLITICS

DERRIDA AND DE MAN

> One shouldn't complicate things for the pleasure of complicating, but one should also never simplify or pretend to be sure of such simplicity where there is none. If things were simple, word would have gotten round, as you say in English.
>
> (Derrida 1988: 119)

While Derrida's reading of Austin on literary or fictional performatives is the best known aspect of his engagement with theories of performativity, the engagement continued into his writing on topics including ethics, law and the nature of the political. In particular, his references to Austinian themes and terminology furnished occasions for further exploration of the thought of iterability. Indeed, if the claim that all language must involve a constitutive iterability is to be effectively registered, then a range of important consequences must be accommodated. We have already seen, for example, how certain oft-encountered ways of thinking about the communication of meaning must come into question. In line with this, the deconstructive emphasis on the ways in which the iterable mark is both constitutive of the communication of our meanings or intentions and the means by which that communication is necessarily confounded therefore has ramifications for how we might comprehend the performative utterance as a kind of moral or social commitment. At the same time, the assumption that the speech act in the speech situation has a conventional structure that allows its validity or felicity to be understood as simple conformity to constitutive rules can be put into question by the recognition that conventional systems or institutions are themselves necessarily implicated in an iterability they cannot simply contain. The exploration of implications such as these is arguably a more thought-provoking aspect of the deconstructive investigation of performativity than the more commonly cited discussion of seriousness, and it is such implications that will be pursued in this chapter. Those unfamiliar with Derrida's work will also be able to see in his working through of iterability an exemplary instance of the kinds of conceptual movement, concerns and implications characteristic of the deconstruction with which his name will always be associated.

INTENTIONALITY AND ITERABILITY

Insofar as Derrida sets the iterability of the linguistic mark against the self-presence or coherence of a meaning or a conscious intention, his account too would appear to reproduce an opposition between intention and convention. In fact, though, the implications of iterability for both concepts are more complicated than this. For a start, iterability does not simply oppose language or the mark to intention. Derrida explicitly allows that there must continue to be some reference to intention even in his model of the performative. If the consequence of his deconstruction is to leave speech acts cut adrift from any ultimate anchoring in a unified meaning or intention, this need not equate to the claim that we simply can't know what a speaker's intentions are when he or she opens his or her mouth, or that such intentions are essentially private and inaccessible. Neither is it the claim that the intentions of a dead or absent writer are unknown or unknowable because he or she is not available to explain them to us. These would be epistemological or epistemic claims, claims about what we can in principle or do in fact know. Derrida quite clearly dissociated his argument from such claims, but they have nonetheless often been attributed to him (Derrida 1988: 56, 65–66; Searle 1977:

202; Searle 1994: 660–62. See also, for example, Skinner 1988: 280–81).
Instead, Derrida suggests that in the deconstructed account of the speech
act, 'the category of intention will not disappear; it will have its place,
but from that place it will no longer be able to govern the entire scene
and system of utterance' (Derrida 1988: 18). That place cannot now be
that of a self-present idea or meaning that is communicated in the speech
situation of a valid or standard performative utterance. The intentionality of the performative is instead given its chance by the very iterability
that prevents it from being finally or fully actualised. The iterability of
the mark underlies my ability to say what I want to say, but at the same
time and in the same movement it limits it at its inception for all the
reasons outlined in the previous chapter. Intentionality therefore keeps
its place in the scene of utterance as a movement or drive towards a state
of settled actualisation that cannot quite be reached, but it cannot be
appealed to as the source or essence of the performative.

So intentionality ought not to be understood as that which ani-
mates or gives life to the otherwise inert conventional procedures of
language, procedures that are held to do nothing unless thus animated.
Derrida argues that iterability is also inside intentionality: there
could be no 'speaker meaning' without it or apart from it. And iterability, as we have seen, cannot be thought of as a kind of presence or unity
or plenitude: it is instead an internal difference, the necessary possibility
of a rupture or a break. So the picture that Derrida paints of the relation
between the conventionality of the procedure and the intentionality of
the speaker does not pit them against one another or see them as
external to each other. The relationship that he posits is much more
dynamic than a static opposition of different kinds, as we can see if we
take up one of the ways in which the difference has sometimes been
imagined. In the suggestion that intentions give life to the inert conventions of language we find a not uncommon view of our relation to
language: we have our living, human purposes or meanings, and language is the tool or technology that we use to pursue them. It is itself
impersonal, inanimate or mechanical; it is secondary, derivative, a set of
procedures invented by the living and put to use to further their
primary purposes. Yet in Derrida's model such a view cannot be maintained: iterability forces on us the disturbing thought that something
technical or mechanical haunts our purposes and meanings at their
origin.

PERFORMATIVITY AND TECHNICITY

In fact, the thinking of the performative from Austin onwards is inflected by a sense of language as somehow machine-like. If machines are understood not only as the tools of human purposes but as means for producing standardised outputs according to repeatable and regular sequences of operations or moves, then the speech act considered in its conventional aspect might claim some affinity with the machine. Such a comparison perhaps seems a little strained or outlandish: if so, we should remind ourselves that this definition of the machine encompasses not just obviously technological processes but also activities we might consider more abstract, like the basic computations of a calculator or even the more advanced procedures of a game of chess. Certainly, Austin's suggestion that speaking involves operating in accordance with conventional procedures, and that the normativity of language depends in part on reference to such procedures, could be read as the invocation of a machinic model of the performative. Such an understanding underpins the distinction between perlocutionary and illocutionary aspects of the performative: whereas the former is a matter of chance for Austin, something that is not predictable or regular, the latter's taking place is precisely a matter of invoking a proper procedure in proper circumstances. Seen from this viewpoint, the conventional rules and procedures that constitute a wedding, say, amount to a machine for making marriages.

Yet the machine can also be that which works automatically, by itself, without the animating input of a user's living hand. This is partly why machines can seem threatening as well as useful, why science fiction narratives are often eloquent on the horrors of computers or robots that slip out of control and develop a life of their own. Such a life is empty, a semblance or image of what it is to be alive, but nonetheless disturbingly akin to life itself: machines of this sort therefore give shape to an archetypal set of fears about the perilously insecure boundary between the organic and the technical, fears given their modern embodiment in everything from the monster of Mary Shelley's *Frankenstein* to the Replicants in Philip K. Dick's *Do Androids Dream of Electric Sheep?* and Ridley Scott's *Bladerunner*, the computer HAL in Stanley Kubrick's *2001: A Space Odyssey*, and the Daleks and Cybermen of the BBC television series, *Doctor Who*. These fears are themselves all the more insistent because they are the necessary accompaniment of the invention of this kind of machine, which gains this uncanny quasi-life precisely by virtue of being automatic. If automata are unnerving, it is because their automaticity allows them to trespass on the territory of the living without properly belonging to it. Thus, the computer and the android can all too easily be imagined as mad or murderous because their very machinic qualities are already threatening: they have all the power and the appearance of life without the standpoint or the soul of the living. They are always more undead than alive.

The performative as the inanimate tool of our purposes recalls the first aspect of this definition of the machine. Yet Austin's suggestion that 'our word is our bond', that to speak is to be opened up to normative requirements whether we like it or not, goes some way towards investing the speech act with an automaticity that is rather less comfortably imagined. If the taking place of the performative can thus be likened to the automatic *performance* of a machine, difficulties ensue: principally, the equally central idea that the performative utterance belongs to and affects a speaker and his or her interlocutors, that it is *meaningful* in just this way, would appear to be threatened by such a likeness. As Derrida puts it, considering the performative utterance as an instance of a commitment taken on:

> Performativity will never be reduced to technical performance. Pure performativity implies the presence of a living being, and of a living being speaking one time only, in its own name, in the first person. And speaking in a manner that is at once spontaneous, intentional, free, and irreplaceable.
>
> (Derrida 2002a: 74)

For Derrida, this aspect of the performative will have to be thought not against the conception of language as technical or machinic, but instead *through* it. If the iterability of the mark is itself a kind of technicity, then it underlies the possibility of the performative as meaningful event even as it also prevents it from being 'pure' in the way suggested in this passage. The theory of the performative must once again confront the troubled combination of apparently irreconcilable but equally necessary aspects or elements.

DE MAN ON ROUSSEAU: THE SPEECH ACT OF EXCUSE

In one of his later engagements with these issues Derrida takes his bearings from an essay by the Belgian-American formulator of another, similarly distinctive pattern of deconstructive reading, Paul de Man (see Derrida 2002a: 71–160). De Man was a highly influential and controversial figure in literary studies during the seventies and early eighties, a leading member of the 'Yale school' of deconstructive critics that also included Geoffrey Hartman and J. Hillis Miller. A few years after his death in 1983 articles that the young de Man had contributed to a collaborationist newspaper in occupied Belgium during the Second World War came to light; a new controversy was then sparked by the polemical attempts of some critics to suggest that deconstruction in general was compromised by this shameful juvenilia (see Hamacher, Hertz and Keenan 1989). A frequently heard accusation was that deconstruction's questioning of the presuppositions upon which philosophical or theoretical certainties could be built was merely nihilistic, a way of avoiding pressing political or moral demands that could itself be read in the light of de Man's wartime collaboration, as an attempt to excuse it. Such a critique misses its target: deconstruction is not nihilism, and it does not suspend or evade reference to politics or ethics. The opposite is in fact the case: although the work of neither Derrida nor de Man could be said to amount to the espousal of a particular set of political or ethical positions, as if it were a kind of party manifesto or ten point plan, the way in which deconstruction pursues the consequences of its engagement with Austin demonstrates a heightened sense of the unavoidable relevance of both political and ethical contexts.

De Man's most relevant contributions are to be found in his *Allegories of Reading*, a series of close analyses of literary and philosophical texts that enacts his distinctive setting out of the ways in which such readings, and reading in general, fail to come to an end in a final or unified 'meaning' (de Man 1979). De Man's concern is to show how reading involves the resort to aspects of textuality that remain as mutually incompatible as they are inextricable from each other. Reading is not, therefore, the business of arriving at a single or final understanding of the text, the kind of understanding that could rest fulfilled in its mastery: it is rather a matter of tracing out the necessary sequence of irreconcilable moves or moments on which a text depends, and therefore of failing to end up at a position from which the different moments or moves could all be comprehended at once or as one. Among the works he reads in this fashion are a number by the eighteenth century Franco-Swiss philosopher and writer, Jean-Jacques Rousseau, including his intriguing, posthumously published *Confessions*, in which Rousseau writes of his formative experiences. One of the best known episodes in the *Confessions* is an incident in which the young Rousseau, having stolen a ribbon, attempts to clear his name by himself accusing Marion, a maid who works for the household in which he is also employed. In de Man's account, Rousseau's confessional narrative serves both to accuse and to excuse his younger self (de Man 1979: 278–301), appealing in explanation of his conduct to two very different elements in the situation. On the one hand, an appeal is made to the convoluted psychological motivations that underpinned the accusation of Marion, in which it is made to appear that it was precisely his regard for the girl that caused Rousseau to attempt to frame her. On the other hand, his accusation of her is portrayed as something he did without thinking and without motivation, the name 'Marion' therefore being produced at the crucial moment without forethought or intention. 'I excused myself,' Rousseau says, 'upon the first thing that offered itself' (de Man 1979: 288).

De Man's reading sees in these contrasting appeals, and in the sudden and unmotivated shift between them, a working together of two irreconcilable ways of understanding language. The psychological narrative unfurls a complex series of substitutions governed by the psychic forces of desire and repression, in which the ribbon comes to stand for Rousseau's desire for Marion, and his seemingly barbarous and cowardly accusation can therefore be understood as the outcome of the workings of these forces. In de Man's reading, this level of explication is complemented by one in which the process of confession is itself subjected to the play of these forces. All such accounts, though, depend on an understanding of Rousseau's actions as making sense, however tortuous, pathological or convoluted: if he accused Marion, and if he is now confessing to having done so, then these actions can be comprehended as processes linked in an undeniably complex, but ultimately meaningful, psychological story. There may be strange figurative moves, in which the ribbon and the name 'Marion' come to stand metaphorically for other things, but even these figurative substitutions make the kind of psychological sense that dreams of falling or going to work naked are often presumed to make: the metaphors can be resolved into their underlying literal meanings, and they can in this way be interpreted satisfactorily and conclusively.

The shift to the other kind of appeal, though, challenges this whole order of explanation. If Rousseau's accusation of Marion was not a link in a meaningful or motivated chain of actions, but the purest of accidents, his alighting on the nearest object to hand, then the accusation and the excuse are of a very different kind. On the one hand, he has here the best of all possible excuses for accusing Marion. He simply didn't mean it: the word that fell from his mouth was just an empty sound, not an accusation at all. As de Man puts it:

> It is only if the act that initiated the entire chain, the utterance of the sound 'Marion', is truly without any conceivable motive that the total arbitrariness of the action becomes the most effective, the most efficaciously performative excuse of all. The estrangement between subject and utterance is then so radical that it escapes any mode of comprehension. When everything else fails, one can always plead insanity. 'Marion' is meaningless and powerless to generate by itself the chain of causal substitutions and figures that structures the surrounding text. . . . It stands entirely out of the system of truth, virtue, and understanding (or of deceit, evil, and error) that gives meaning to the passage.
>
> (De Man 1979: 289)

Rousseau's appeal, de Man suggests, is to language as a kind of automatic machine that performs its functions independently of subjective investments:

> The chain of substitutions functions next to another, differently structured system that exists independently of referential determination, in a system that is both entirely arbitrary and entirely repeatable, like a grammar.
>
> (De Man 1979: 300)

Because language can do this, because it can work automatically and without reference to conscious human purposes, then the real scandal of his accusation is that everyone took it as such. His utterance of the sound 'Marion' wasn't meant as accusation because it wasn't *meant* at all.

And insofar as this sense of 'not meaning it' can be sustained, then it exemplifies the 'radical irresponsibility of fiction' (de Man 1979: 293), an irresponsibility that ought to render such exemplary fictional utterances harmless or innocent.

'AN EXPLODING MACHINE'

Yet for de Man's Rousseau to excuse himself by thus invoking the machinic workings of language is not as simply effective as might at first be thought. Such an invocation also ruins the excuse it makes possible, since it disconnects Rousseau not only from guilt but also from innocence, indeed from the whole spectrum of ethical considerations or responsibilities into which it intrudes. As Derrida says, 'automatic and mechanical pardons and excuses cannot have the value of pardon and excuse' (Derrida 2002a: 134): speaking cannot here be the proper process of putting on moral responsibilities, since the linguistic process of generating those commitments is machinic and indifferent. For this reason, de Man suggests, the machine model of language in Rousseau's work is perceived as a threat to the conscious self whose moral life, from another perspective, is lived through language:

> Writing always includes the moment of dispossession in favour of the arbitrary power play of the signifier and from the point of view of the subject, this can only be experienced as a dismemberment, a beheading or a castration.
>
> (De Man 1979: 296)

This 'arbitrary power play' is precisely language's power to work automatically: the conscious subject, the language user, experiences this moment as a radical undoing. It is now simply caught up in the workings of the machine, threatened with the inevitable mutilations suffered by those unfortunate enough to suffer such a fate. The machine generates all the scenes of what ought to be a subjective moral life, all the stagings of guilt, innocence, accusation and excuse. Yet the subject of this moral life is now dragged along as the victim of the scenes that the machine creates all by itself.

De Man's reading, though, does not resolve itself around this machine model, or the opposition between it and the prior reading in terms of motive, meaning and morals. Instead, he sees the two view-points on language here developed as implicated in each other without the possibility of a final, totalising resolution. For a start, to invoke the machine model as the point at which the reading comes to a stop would be to install it as the final meaning of the text, and therefore to lapse back into the other picture from which the reading set out. So de Man prefers to suggest that Rousseau's text *enacts* the interplay between these two aspects, that it is in motion between or across them. His reading traces this enactment, which is therefore a kind of performance or tak-ing place irreducible to any ultimate statement or final meaning. And this performance is what characterises text as such for de Man, as he says in another essay:

> We call *text* any entity that can be considered from such a double per-spective: as a generative, open-ended, non-referential grammatical system [i.e., as a machine] and as a figural system closed off by a transcendental signification [i.e. as a linked chain of metaphors trace-able to a final or literal meaning] that subverts the grammatical code to which the text owes its existence.
>
> (De Man 1979: 270)

That the one system *subverts* the other means that the performance a text undertakes is not single or simple, but restless and multiple. The text is therefore best imagined not as an organic, coherent entity, something entire of and enclosed in itself, but as a kind of endless work: it might still be apprehended as a machine, but a machine now that is not simply regular or predictable, one that instead *performs* the interference between these different aspects of textuality. These systems, de Man argues, are incompatible, and one cannot be reduced to the other; yet there would not be what we call text or language without *both* of them. In this dou-ble perspective the text is, as one of de Man's most perceptive readers has put it, 'an exploding machine . . . A machine for exploding, a machine that explodes' (Chase 1986: 9).

GETTING AWAY WITH IT

The de Manian account of textuality is one of the resources on which Derrida draws in order to give some shape to the difficult combination of irreconcilable aspects or moments that he finds in the thinking of the performative. The peculiar performance of the text to which de Man points is reminiscent of the peculiarities in Derrida's own notion of iterability. As we saw above, that notion requires the re-examination of the basis on which differences crucial to the elaboration of speech act theory, such as that between the intentional and the conventional aspects of the performative, might be understood. Derrida's interventions repeatedly suggested that iterability was both the condition of the possibility of a proper speech act, and at the same time – in the same move – the condition of its impossibility. Iterability, in other words, is both a necessary presupposition of the theory of performativity, and also that which ensures that the felicity of any attempted performative could not simply be accounted for by reference to the enabling conditions set out by any comprehensive theory of speech acts. In generating such an unavoidably contradictory outcome, iterability marks what Derrida called an *aporia*, a blockage or impasse in thinking. When de Man suggests that his '"definition" of the text also states the impossibility of its existence' (de Man 1979: 270) he is gesturing towards the same kind of obligation to think the strictly unthinkable, of trying like Derrida to explicate a 'law of undecidable contamination' that reveals the unavoidable dependence on each other of incompatible concepts. The conceptual network of speech act theory is one site of such necessary contamination, and it is therefore a contamination that affects the attempt to provide an account of how language is involved in establishing our commitments and responsibilities. As we shall see, this kind of contamination need not mark the end of such attempts: it can also point to other ways of thinking such things.

So both de Man and Derrida find in the exploration of the performative resources for troubling rather than settling fundamental questions about language and its use; as part of this, both also see as particularly interesting the suggestion of a kind of 'performativity' that might not simply invoke the conformity of an utterance to a set of felicity conditions. In chapter three we saw how Searle's class of declarations could be described as a kind of 'linguistic magic', the last redoubt of a 'pure' performativity: they were the kind of utterance where saying did indeed, all by itself, make something happen. Acknowledging this, Searle himself later reserved the name 'performative' for declarations (see Searle 1989: 536). This kind of performativity was itself *constitutive*: it brought something about or made something happen. For both Austin and

Searle, though, this power or force would seem to be a function of existing felicity conditions: my words can adjourn a meeting, open a new hospital, name a child or launch a ship only if I say the right thing in the right circumstances, and if I am the right person to say it. Otherwise, the change that such a performative could make in the world remains unmade. Yet Austin, at least, also acknowledges that the inventive or constitutive force of the declarative might happen without such existing conditions, in 'the case of procedures which someone is initiating', a possibility he described as 'get[ting] away with it' (Austin 1975: 30). And Cavell speaks of words as projected into new contexts, taking on new implications, functioning in unanticipated ways. While Austin leaves this possibility unexplored, Derrida is more acutely concerned to factor it into the picture he is seeking to paint.

A couple of examples will serve to illustrate how this kind of questioning unfolds. That paradigmatic speech act, the promise, has as one of its felicity conditions the fulfilment of what is promised. If I promise to tell you something, that promise cannot be fully felicitous until such time as I actually keep it. Imagine, for example, that we are friends who have not seen much of each other recently; you bump into me in the street one day, and I promise to give you a call some time. There are, perhaps, reasons for you to expect that this wasn't really a promise: I was in a bit of a rush when I said it, or I don't have a good record of keeping my word in this way. But then I do make the call: at that point, and only at that point, the 'promise' can be confirmed as a promise, a commitment that changes our relation to each other. There is, in other words, an irreducibly temporal aspect to the promise: it looks forward to its own felicity. Yet at the same time, for the promise to come into effect, for it to make a difference to both you and me, the question of its felicity cannot be postponed in this fashion: this is why we say that the promise commits us as soon as it is issued, and that it commits us precisely to doing what we promised. Furthermore, because the promise commits me to doing something in the future, it can be offered ever so freely and easily. And if the determination of its felicity depends on how the world will be, rather than how it is, there can be no way (yet) of telling an infelicitous one from its felicitous counterpart (see Felman 2002: 32–40).

This is the difficulty that Searle tries to escape by insisting on the importance of my intention at the moment that I speak as a prime determinant of validity; but if the felicity of any speech act involves the invocation of a speech situation understood more broadly than this, then the issue is not to be so easily evaded. There is no promise that is not taken on trust by both its issuer and its receiver, *as if* it were indeed the promise it claimed to be. Its temporal structure fractures the unified moment of the speech situation, making it both forward-looking and retroactive. Think, for example, of the paper money we use. The Bank of England ten pound note in my wallet actually declares itself to be a promise to pay me ten pounds if I present it at the issuing bank. If I do so, though, I will be given another note inscribed with the same promise. I cannot actually get at what is promised: this particular speech situation is endlessly extended. But this proleptic way in which the promise gets ahead of itself, this requirement to take it on trust, does not stop it from functioning in the world in the most material way. A promise, in other words, is risky or excessive: it has illocutionary force before or beyond any demonstration or confirmation of its felicity (Derrida 1989a: 93–94). Its validity, in other words, cannot be just a matter of its conformity to set procedures – somehow, something else is involved.

This difficulty can also be posed in another fashion and with further consequences. Most paper money is what is called 'fiat money': its value as money results from the declarative act, the fiat, of an institution such as a bank or a government. The English ten pound note can do its institutional work because it is underpinned by the institutional authority of English law, which itself is only valid if it is made in the appropriate fashion. Insofar as the felicity of each speech act is a function of its conformity to existing conditions, in other words, it rests on a prior speech act, which in turn rests on a prior speech act, all the way down. But all the way down to where? Where can it stop? The whole process must have a beginning: but where can we find a set of felicity conditions for a speech act that do not depend in some way on the speech act of their own institution? And if we do eventually reach an instance of a speech act managing to get away with it like this, to furnish itself with the conditions of its own felicity, then what does that say about any appeal to the conventional aspect of linguistic normativity? What is at stake here, in other words, is precisely the possibility of legitimacy or validity, the appeal to a set of conventions as the matrix of such normativity. How could it make sense to talk of an impossible performativity, a sort of constitutive declaration, beyond or before such conventions? How could there be a reference to validity or felicity that did not involve the invocation of the kinds of authorising rules or procedures that this legal or constitutional scene involves?

'ORIGINARY PERFORMATIVITY': THE DECLARATION OF INDEPENDENCE

Derrida found an opportunity to explore such questions further in a brief but important analysis of the American Declaration of Independence of 1776, one of the most central works of Western political history. Given its title, this text might be thought to fall unproblematically within a recognisable class of speech acts, precisely those which are capable of bringing something about in speaking of it. After an extensive preamble outlining the circumstances and occasion of the speech act, the actual declaration itself takes a textbook form:

> We, therefore, the Representatives of the United States Of America, in General Congress, Assembled, appealing to the Supreme Judge of the World for the Rectitude of our Intentions, do, in the Name, and by Authority of the good People of these Colonies, solemnly Publish and Declare, That these United Colonies are, and of Right ought to be, Free And Independent States; that they are absolved from all Allegiance to the British Crown, and that all political Connection between them and the State of Great-Britain, is and ought to be totally dissolved; and that as Free And Independent States, they have full Power to levy War, conclude Peace, contract Alliances, establish Commerce, and to do all other Acts and Things which Independent States may of right do.

Insofar as a declaration such as this is a pure performative, a piece of linguistic magic that conjures up the state of affairs to which it refers, then what we have here is the actual taking place of a political, world-historical, undeniably factual event. The moment when the declaration that 'these United Colonies are . . . Free and Independent States' is issued is the moment that their independence is produced, that colonies become states, much as the adjournment of a meeting would happen, as an event, at the very moment when the appropriate person declared, 'the meeting is adjourned'.

Yet there is still an issue here, which Derrida begins to explore by asking who the 'We' that speaks here actually is. By what right is this declaration issued? On what grounds could this be judged a felicitous event, a speech act with illocutionary force? The declaration itself refers to its speakers, those who sign their names to this utterance and in so doing claim it as theirs, as 'Representatives'. Although they sign, therefore, they are standing in for others when they do so, signing in their name. And the others for whom they are signing, whose 'Authority' they represent, are 'the good People of these Colonies'. It is 'the People' who have licensed this act, and who are the ultimate actors behind it. The problem, though, is that the status of this 'People' is hard to determine. The declaration would seem to suggest that the People and their authority precedes it: if they are somehow able now to issue performatives through their representatives, then they themselves must be already validly *constituted as* a people, as the kind of entity capable of felicitously appointing representatives, or having others sign in its singular name. On this condition, the use of the word 'people' in this declaration would be constative or descriptive, what Searle calls an assertive: when it speaks of the people, the declaration is merely referring to an entity that exists already, prior to the declaration itself. But, as Derrida points out, 'these people', its ultimate signatories, 'do not exist' prior to the issuing of the declaration itself:

> They do *not* exist as an entity, the entity does *not* exist *before* this declaration, not *as such.* If it [i.e. the 'people'] gives birth to itself, as free and independent subject, as possible signer, this can hold only in the act of signature. The signature invents the signer.
>
> (Derrida 2002b: 49)

The declaration, that is to say, actually *produces* the people as an entity: it constitutes the state of affairs of which it speaks. And it is only by means of this declaration, this magical performative, that some of the colonial subjects of King George III become a 'free and independent' People capable of authorising representatives to act in its name. This has a couple of interesting consequences. Firstly, here we have an occasion on which the ultimate speaker of an utterance, in this case the 'people', has itself been invented by the utterance issued. Instead of the collective speaker coming first, and then issuing its utterances as the product of its general will or shared intention, the speaker is retroactively constituted by the utterance it appears to authorise. In an uncanny fashion the speech act speaks itself, and in doing so speaks of the speaking 'people' it invents. One could perhaps say that such an utterance is another promise of the sort outlined above. It is an utterance that can be felicitous only to the extent that it looks backwards and forwards, only to the extent that it manages to promise that there will have been a speaker.

The second consequence also arises from this sense of a strange temporal displacement at work in the declaration. It refers back to the people that authorises it, but also looks forward to that people as the entity it will constitute through its utterance: the text is therefore both an appeal to existing felicity conditions, and an attempt to institute those conditions. The validity or felicity of the declaration is dependent on its being both these things at once, on a kind of split in itself that makes its taking place a paradoxical and frankly impossible occurrence. The point is, though, that without this impossibility there could be no validity. It is only because of this difference from itself, what Derrida calls 'this indispensable confusion' at its heart, that it could possibly be felicitous (Derrida 2002b: 51). This is not to suggest that the USA or any other institution is in some way invalid, and all its rights merely usurped. It is just to point out that the invocation of an already existing 'People' as a prior source of validity for the declarations of its representatives both underpins *and* conceals the peculiar invention of such an entity, the event of its taking place. In fact, it underpins it *because* it conceals it. This is a 'confusion' because it implies a speech act that fails to conform to proper felicity conditions, and indeed seems to violate any appeal to the consistency of a single speech situation; it is 'indispensable' because no felicitous declaration could take place without it. Without both these moments, the declaration could not possibly be valid; with them, impossibly, it is.

This founding moment, then, seeks to produce an institution or set of institutions, an entity made up of rules, conventions, laws and procedures of the sort to which Searle's reading and appropriation of Austin, in particular, appeals to justify its sense of how the pragmatic validity of utterance is determined. The 'United States of America' is a rule-governed entity of this kind, as are other political institutions, universities, football leagues, currencies, even natural or ordinary languages. But the impossible scene of its institution, in which its founders appeal for the validity of their right and power to declare to the prior existence of the very entity, the 'people', that they presume to create when they speak, shows how all such rights and powers, all such claims to legal or procedural validity, depend on the doubleness of an impossible founding act. All institutions must ultimately be traceable to an original moment, the moment of their invention, yet the beginning must have this differential nature, this original split in its taking place that opens it at the outset to what is other than the purely conventional (see also Derrida 1989b: 25–65).

So in this situation, the illocutionary force that characterises an act performed rightfully, according to prior conditions or authorisation, is intertwined with a more violent force that serves to validate the act by splitting it from itself. The first kind of force is a function of an institutional framework of conventions that accords validity to acts performed through this framework: it is this that allows us to distinguish rightful or effective marriage ceremonies, for example, from their parodic, nonbinding or invalid opposites. If the second kind of force can be described as violent it is not because weaponry, physical force or assaults on the citadels of power are necessarily involved. It is violent only because this force is not simply derived from conformity to prior felicity conditions. Derrida's analysis shows that such different kinds of force do not finally, or even originally, exclude each other, and that there can therefore be no pure legitimacy. For this reason, he refers to such founding or inventive acts as manifesting an illocutionary force of a distinctive, seemingly impossible kind:

> [an] originary performativity that does not conform to preexisting conventions, unlike all the performatives analyzed by the theoreticians of speech acts, but whose force of *rupture* produces the institution or the constitution, the law itself, which is to say also the meaning that appears to, that ought to, or that appears to have to guarantee it in return.
>
> (Derrida 1994: 30–31)

Or as he puts it elsewhere:

> This moment calls for new conventions which it itself proposes or promises, but which, for that reason, it cannot without artifice take advantage of or found its authority on at the very moment that it calls for new laws.
>
> (Derrida 1989a:119)

If this is a rupture, it is both the rupture from any conventions or institutions that might precede such an originary performative, and also, crucially, the rupture *within* the event of the foundational speech act, that difference from itself that is crucial to its validity. So such 'originary' performativity cannot simply function before or beyond the illocutionary force that depends on the regularity of conventions or procedures. Rather, it inhabits it: it is the openness to inventiveness, to that which is yet to come, which is always at work in any conventional structure.

FORCE, CONVENTIONS AND THE POLICE

To speak of this kind of openness, this 'originary performativity', as a *rupture* is to flag up its relation to the iterability that has been the organising motif of Derrida's encounter with Austin and Searle. In setting out the features of iterability Derrida characterised it as a *'force de rupture'*, 'a force that breaks with the collectivity of presences organizing the moment of its inscription' (Derrida 1988: 9). Thus he is able to show how the iterability that prevents us from positing a neat, effective theoretical distinction between standard and non-standard utterances, or from cleanly contrasting intentionality and conventionality, is also turned on appeals made by speech act theory to the validating power of conventions, rules or codes themselves. This is a point that Derrida makes early on in his initial essay: because the iterable mark must be capable of breaking with any context, and being grafted into new contexts, it is also always capable of opening the code of which it is part to an as yet unimagined future. The iterability that is essential to the elements of such systems is precisely the constant possibility of new and different systems. No set of conventions, therefore, will ever be able ultimately to close on itself; no code can ever be assumed to be complete or properly bounded (Derrida 1988: 9). Furthermore, these are also the grounds for suggesting that the illocutionary force derived from the conformity of an act to the code that establishes its effectiveness or validity cannot simply be opposed to the force that I have here called violence. This kind of force is not the *product* of conventional systems: it is instead that which both makes such systems possible, since there could be no conventions without iterable marks capable of functioning beyond any particular context, and yet on the same conditions prevents them from establishing or securing themselves as *properly* systematic.

But still there *are* apparently finite or stable systems of conventions, or functioning institutions, and there *are* both 'serious' performatives and their 'fictional' counterparts. Valid weddings take place, while fictional ones are enacted on stage or in films; universities teach, examine and award degrees; nation-states have elections, declare wars and negotiate international treaties. Money continues to make the world go round. If, as Derrida says, the ways that speech act theories try to account for the distinctions between these kinds of act or entity cannot be sustained, then how are we to account for them? Does deconstruction leave us in the position of having to deny the existence or, rather, the taking place of the most obvious, ordinary things? Derrida, as we might expect, did not think so. If the distinction between felicitous and infelicitous speech acts is shown to be undecidable, then that doesn't mean that we cannot speak of such a distinction, or that it cannot be made. It simply means that the account of its making offered by speech act theory depends on its own necessary, but unacknowledged, fictions. The undecidability that Derrida's analysis of speech act theory shows up does not cancel or prevent the drawing of the distinction. It means, rather, that the distinction does not just emerge, as it were, as an inevitable or automatic consequence of the workings of a conventional structure. Instead, the drawing of any distinction is precisely *a decisive instance*: it is an interruption of the conventional apparatus on which the apparatus must depend, but which it can neither ground nor easily acknowledge. The deconstructive analysis thus points out that no system of conventions can ever be entire of itself, that such systems presuppose decisions for which responsibility must be taken (Derrida 1988: 116). These are not decisions that follow automatically from, or are underpinned by, an already existing rule or convention. A 'decision' that simply followed a set procedure would not be worthy of the name. So instead of a picture that shows our commitments arising from speech acts that are themselves underpinned by systematic conventions, Derrida reveals an ethical situation in which our responsibilities exceed any such systematic accounting.

In advancing this claim, Derrida's work queries the basic assumptions of speech act theory regarding the conventional or rule-governed nature of language considered as an institution (Derrida 1988: 19). This kind of work could expose the aspiration for a systematic account to the ethical situation suggested here, an exposure that would sustain a deconstructive questioning of the appeal to rules, procedures or laws. Yet the appearance of this kind of undecidability can also involve an attempt to reassert and impose the system of rules it affects. As Derrida suggests:

> Ultimately there is always a police and a tribunal ready to intervene each time that a rule . . . is invoked . . . If the police is always waiting in the wings, it is because conventions are *by essence* violable and precarious.
>
> (Derrida 1988: 105; my emphasis)

This kind of 'police' is not necessarily uniformed and carrying batons. Even a language can be supplemented by a police: in France, as Derrida points out, the Académie Française not only claims for itself the right to determine valid French usage but also seeks to prohibit usages that break its rules (Derrida 1988: 135). This kind of agency would be one that insists upon the rules, interrupting and arresting the iterability that also serves both to make such rules possible and to threaten in advance their integrity or purity as rules. So deconstruction makes any appeal to the convention or the constitutive rule as the matrix of illocutionary validity extremely problematic. 'Conventionality' is not, now, a secure concept or value to which we can refer if we wish to explain how we do things with language or how our responsibilities and commitments arise. From this position, to say that institutions of all sorts are 'systems of conventions', and that discursive events are the products of such systems, cannot be the last word in explaining how their effects are achieved. But this is not simply because forces or agencies entirely separate from such systems would need to be considered as well. Rather, the explanation in terms of conventionality contains its own presuppositions, and it is these that the deconstructive analysis seeks to set out, explore and unsettle.

THE FUNCTION OF THEORY

What, then, are the implications of such an analysis for understanding speech act theory's attempts to comprehend language's illocutionary dimension? Is it merely falsified in its deconstruction? Not really: in fact, an important implication of Derrida's analysis is that such a theory's place in the process of policing is brought out and clarified. By demonstrating that vital distinctions such as that between serious and non-serious performatives are not logically secured through the process of theorisation, deconstruction points out the degree to which such a theory itself is involved in staging the kind of decisive intervention into the undecidable analysed above. Yet in the account it gives of itself, a speech act theory such as Searle's does not recognise that it is doing any such thing: it is not *instituting* and enforcing a distinction between seriousness and parasitism, it is merely *describing* its logical basis. Its police work is therefore thoroughly dissimulated: it is working undercover. The substance of the distinctions on which it insists is, it claims, simply unarguable: thus, for Searle, the fictional is to the serious speech act as the secondary is to the primary, the imitation to the imitated, the pretended to the actual. It is, as we saw in chapter four, in a relation of 'logical dependence' (Searle 1977: 205). Yet if Derrida's account of iterability holds then this claim to have articulated the *logical* basis of the distinction cannot be upheld, and, as we have already seen, a dogmatic moment is revealed. If the primary can be shown to be in an equally dependent relation to the secondary, then the stipulations of speech act theory are shown to be far from unarguable or logically secured. In that case, we now have reason enough to question the way in which the distinction has been drawn.

As far as Derrida is concerned, this insight takes us right into some of the fundamental structures not just of speech act theory but of Western philosophy in general, and indeed into the very idea of 'fundamental structures'. Insofar as a theory of speech acts assumes that the only way to proceed philosophically is to return 'to an origin or to a "priority" held to be simple, intact, normal, pure, standard, self-identical, in order then to think in terms of derivation, complication, deterioration, accident', then it is drawing on those structures:

> All metaphysicians, from Plato to Rousseau, Descartes to Husserl, have proceeded in this way, conceiving good to be before evil, the positive before the negative, the pure before the impure, the simple before the complex, the essential before the accidental, the imitated before the imitation, etc.
>
> (Derrida 1988: 93)

The broader work of a deconstructive writing is to unsettle precisely this set of fundamental structures, these conceptual oppositions in which one pole of the opposition is presumed to be full, substantial or central and therefore to come first. Across the bulk of his early and most influential work, Derrida seeks to show more broadly what he has claimed to demonstrate here: that the philosophical enterprise, even at its most basic, depends on unthought or dogmatic moments that it cannot recognise as such.

What, then, is deconstruction's place in the general enterprise of theory, the enterprise of which a theory of performativity might be thought to be a part? Does it have any significant relation to this project that it strives so persistently to unsettle? On the one hand, it must do so if it is to have any purchase on it at all. Derrida's claim is always that the deconstruction of the philosophical texts his work analyses is something that they do to themselves: they are deconstructed by following out the network of presuppositions that they conceal in their exposition. On the other hand, deconstruction cannot simply be another theory or another kind of philosophy since so many of the basic assumptions of theory and philosophy are vulnerable to being opened up in this fashion. For example, it would be wrong to think of Derrida's account of theories of the performative as another, more thoroughgoing attempt to produce a comprehensive, systematic theory of the essence of performativity. This is not an effort to establish a new basis or foundation which could properly satisfy anyone's systematic or idealising ambitions. It is, rather, work towards exposing the thought of the 'basis' or 'system' to what it cannot think, or to what it has not yet thought, to the otherness or futurity already at work in its thinking. Iterability installed the breach, hollowness or absence that speech act theory tried to think of as a secondary accident at the heart of the concept of the performative. Iterability also ensured that the concept of the performative could not be thought of as a self-identical unity, a meaning or intention or even an element in a code: instead, it is differential, divided at its origin. It is the *sameness* implicit in iterability that makes the concept, as a unified meaning persisting through time and across various contexts, possible; but it can have such sameness only on the basis of a difference, a repeatability, that marks it at its origin and therefore makes it always different from itself or open to the other. For this reason, iterability cannot quite be a concept itself: it is a 'quasi-concept' of the limits of the concept (Derrida 1988: 119).

Such a thing is no doubt very hard to think: indeed, it is at this point in his analysis that Derrida issues the somewhat wry observation that I have cited as the epigraph for this chapter. Yet this kind of difficulty is not mere mystification or a perverse kind of one-upmanship. The deconstructive exploration is instead a 'writing . . . liable to the other, opened to and by the other, to the work of the other', Derrida suggests (Derrida 1989b: 61). Such a 'liability to the other' is a consistent preoccupation of Derrida's thinking, evident particularly in the sustained reflection in his later work on political and ethical matters; indeed, it is itself a kind of ethical demand or responsibility. And the attention that work gives to conceptions of law, justice, hospitality and sovereignty, in particular, is itself indebted to the deconstructive investigation of the nature of institutions and institutional validity undertaken in his engagement with Austin and Searle (Derrida 1989b; 1992a; 1992b; 1994; 1997; 2005; Derrida and Dufourmantelle 2000).

Deconstruction, therefore, is both theoretical and philosophical, while using the resources of both to query their most basic organising assumptions. As de Man suggested, it is for this reason appropriately considered an instance of theory's 'self-resistance' (de Man 1986: 20). Speech act theory of the type elaborated by Searle, given its declared pursuit of a formalised account of language in use, offers a particularly pertinent resource for the demonstration of such self-resistance: the conceptual certainties that might allow a theory of speech acts to be exhaustively explanatory are called into question. It is worth noting, though, that Austin's reluctance to present the account of the performative as a general theory of language, his insistence on placing the normativity of his felicity conditions within the alterable and multiple field of 'ordinary language', rather than trying to imagine performativity as the effect of a comprehensive set of constitutive rules, might well mean that his account should be seen as much more open than it often is (see Felman 2002: 41–47). Cavell's sense, too, that the normativity of language in use is not simply systematically determined or securely contained within the given limits of an established institution, that it may not be reducible to a calculus of rules, that it indeed always involves precisely the risky 'projection' of words into new contexts, would further complicate any attempt to find in this kind of thinking the tendency to the systematic or foundational that deconstruction itself works through.

To this extent, Cavell joins Derrida in understanding his task as a matter of interrupting the philosophical impulse to *sublime* language, to see in it the possibility of purity or final idealisation. For Cavell, ordinary language philosophy is already one of the prime resources for such work; for the Derrida of 'Signature Event Context' it perhaps remains too clearly animated by that subliming impulse, even as its openness is acknowledged. In one of his late essays, though, Derrida suggests that 'one value of [Austin's] works is to have not only resisted but marked the line of resistance to systematic work, to philosophy as formalizing theorization, absolute and closed, freed of its adherences to ordinary language and to so-called natural languages' (Derrida 2002a: 123). While Searle imagined that his own general theory of speech acts was the fitting continuation of Austin's labours, it is perhaps also appropriate to see in Derrida's working out of theory's self-resistance a fidelity to these other tendencies in Austin's understanding of how we do things with words.

6

BEING PERFORMATIVE
BUTLER

> What moves me politically, and that for which I want to make room, is
> the moment in which a subject – a person, a collective – asserts a
> right or entitlement to a livable life when no such prior authorization
> exists, when no clearly enabling convention is in place.
>
> (Butler 2004: 224)

Even as the implications and consequences of the deconstructive
reworking of speech act theory were still being registered and debated
in the academy, a number of theorists more clearly focused on specific
political projects were beginning to see in the concept of the performative
a resource relevant to their own purposes. In particular, 'queer theory'
began to emerge from the conjoining of a feminist theory and politics of
gender, which had always been productively plural in both its analyses and
its activist demands, and burgeoning academic and political concern
with the comprehension and representation of sexuality. Questions
around sexuality had long been a crucial topic for feminist thinking, and
queer theory was concerned in part to rearticulate the relations between
the identity categories of sex, gender and sexuality. In the work of Eve

Kosofsky Sedgwick, for example, such categories were not assumed as stable reference points for thinking about identity. The history of the category 'homosexual', a history that could both confirm and confound the standard heterosexist association between gender and sexual orientation, was an important resource for this kind of questioning since it could show how such categories were produced while also revealing their potential instability. In an article on Henry James, she focused on what she called 'queer performativity', 'a strategy for the production of meaning and being' (Sedgwick 2003: 61) that reflected critically upon dominant assumptions regarding both identity and the powers of language.

This kind of reflection has found its most sustained expression, though, in the work of the American philosopher Judith Butler. In *Gender Trouble*, *Bodies that Matter* and *Excitable Speech*, in particular, she has presented a challenge to feminist theory and politics that puts the concept of the performative centre stage. To say that her recasting of performativity has been influential would be to understate the case by several orders of magnitude: it has generated voluminous commentary and protracted debate, and had a huge impact on the theory and politics of identity in general as well as on an extensive range of academic disciplines. And while the implications and range of her work reach beyond this recasting, as her more recent publications have demonstrated, it remains among the most commonly remarked features of that work.

RETHINKING THE BODY, CHALLENGING IDENTITY: THE DEMANDS OF POLITICS

It was a sense of the pressing requirements of feminist political activism, rather than mere intellectual curiosity, that led Butler to the concept of performativity as a theoretical resource. As she herself put it in *Gender Trouble*:

> Categories of true sex, discrete gender, and specific sexuality have constituted the stable point of reference for a great deal of feminist theory and politics. These constructs of identity serve as the points of epistemic departure from which theory emerges and politics itself is shaped. In the case of feminism, politics is ostensibly shaped to express the interests, the perspectives, of 'women'. But is there a political shape to 'women', as it were, that precedes and prefigures

> the political elaboration of their interests and epistemic point of view?
> How is that identity shaped, and is it a political shaping that takes the
> very morphology and boundary of the sexed body as the ground, sur-
> face or site of cultural inscription? What circumscribes that site as
> 'the female body'? Is 'the body' or 'the sexed body' the firm founda-
> tion on which gender and systems of compulsory sexuality operate?
> Or is 'the body' itself shaped by political forces with strategic interests
> in keeping that body bounded and constituted by the markers of sex?
>
> (Butler 1999: 164)

In other words, the motivating force for a specifically feminist politics
has often been held to be the need to 'speak for' women, to articulate
the interests of women. Yet such a position might depend on certain
presuppositions that could usefully be challenged, since they themselves
might actually serve to support the power regimes that feminism exists
to contest. In particular, it would seem to require reference to 'woman'
as a stable subject for whom feminist politics should seek to speak; yet
any such subject is not just there, or immediately given: she has been
forged both through the intellectual and political work of feminism
itself, and also – more troublingly – through the regimes of power and
ideology it opposes.

Most importantly, the identity of 'woman' has often been held to
make sense, primarily in prefeminist discourses of gender, at three
linked levels, each of which is itself divided in an exclusively binary fashion. There is, first of all, the level of sex or the sexed body, of chromosomes
and anatomy, where the body can properly exhibit characteristics which
are either and only male or female. There is then the level of social or
cultural identity, of gender, in which social selves and their attributes or
characteristics are again properly and exclusively divided between the
masculine and feminine. Finally, there is the level of sexuality or desire,
which is once more organised along binary lines, with men desiring
women and women desiring men. These different levels are themselves
understood as united in the coherent identities of men and women as
integrated subjects, as the kinds of entity that could have collective
interests requiring or deserving political representation. Thus, a female
body is aligned with that which is culturally feminine, and this woman,
as a proper woman, naturally desires men. In some versions of this
model, bodily sex is held to be the ground that determines both gender

and sexuality; in others, all three levels are held to be aspects of a 'true self' that reveals itself simultaneously at all of them (Butler 1999: 30).

FEMINISM, SEX AND GENDER

Unsurprisingly, given the fact that this binary division is usually a hierarchical one in which men and the masculine are seen as dominant or central, and the 'opposite sex' understood as marginal or subordinate, many versions of feminism have sought to challenge the framework it underpins. Butler's concern is that in mounting this challenge feminist theory and politics might still cement in place a way of thinking about gender that preserves some of these assumptions, and thus limit the political endeavour it is claiming to advance. A critical instance of this is Butler's reluctance to settle for feminist reworkings of the binary system of sex-gender-desire outlined above. Some important strands in French feminist philosophy of the 1970s, for instance, had argued that the binarism of sexual difference was primordial, crucial to the establishment of the claims of modern Western rationality. This form of rationality, which claimed to be comprehensive in its scope and universal in its application, proceeded only on the basis of the dissimulated exclusion of woman or the feminine. At the same time, the psychoanalytic scenarios on which some feminist thinking drew incorporated binary sexual difference as a crucial and essentially invariant component of the formation of the psyche: in the formative processes that we go through in order to become the kind of psychically complex entities that we are, sexual difference was an irreducible element. It is precisely this sense of the *foundational* importance of the category that Butler seeks to contest.

A strand of thought especially associated with the French philosopher Simone de Beauvoir shows these categorial issues well, and provides one of the springboards for Butler's own recasting of the situation. De Beauvoir, Butler says, accepts the sexing of the body as either male or female, but denies that such a binary division implies any necessary consequences for what it is, culturally, to be a woman. Sex does not cause gender; so if sex is a fact, a given, then gender remains open to alteration and transformation. What it is to be a woman at that level remains therefore the proper object of political hopes: 'gender is the variable cultural construction of sex, the myriad and open possibilities of cultural meaning occasioned by a sexed body' (Butler 1999: 142).

Butler, though, sees this account as offering both possibilities and problems for feminism. On the one hand, the fact that sex does not determine gender seems ultimately to imply that there need be no link between sexed bodies and gender identities, and therefore no necessary symmetry between the corporeal and the cultural. The cultural identity 'man' might therefore be applied to a female body, and that of 'woman' to a male body; or perhaps, more radically, there might be a proliferation of genders rather than two (Butler 1999: 10, 143). On the other hand, perhaps too much has been conceded in the acceptance of the facticity or givenness of sex. As Butler herself asks,

> What is 'sex' anyway? Is it natural, anatomical, chromosomal, or hormonal, and how is a feminist critic to assess the scientific discourses which purport to establish such 'facts' for us? Does sex have a history? Does each sex have a different history, or histories? Is there a history of how the duality of sex was established, a genealogy that might expose the binary operations as a variable construction? Are the ostensibly natural facts of sex discursively produced by various scientific discourses in the service of other political and social interests?
>
> (Butler 1999: 10)

So what we call 'sex', and distinguish as the pre-cultural component of identity, can perhaps instead be understood as only *culturally designated* as such. The binary division of a bodily sex, that is to say, is not a given but a cultural category; if it is dissimulated as 'nature' in accounts of identity, then feminism ought to challenge this dissimulation, not participate in it. Perhaps then a future beyond the duality of sex would become a political possibility. And this would inevitably have effects on the thinking of sexuality, too. The apparently necessary binary of heterosexuality, the alignment of desire with a natural or given sex, would no longer hold. Ways of desiring beyond the oppressive influence of the heterosexual norm would become possible. But what is then in question is not simply the organisation of these varying components of what can still be settled eventually as an identity. Instead, Butler's more basic strategy is to find ways of 'articulat[ing] the convergence of multiple sexual discourses at the site of "identity" in order to render that category, in whatever form, permanently problematic' (Butler 1999: 163). For this reason, she is drawn to examples and situations that can be seen to cause this kind of trouble for gender identity: in the course of her writings she has drawn attention to the difficulties that do in fact bedevil attempts to trace the binary categories of sexual difference back to an ultimate anatomical or chromosomal source in the body. She has emphasised the difficulties besetting attempts to categorise or medicalise intersex and transsexual people, and sought to explore the significance for a politics of sexuality of varieties of cross-dressing and gender differentiation. Prominent among these have been the practice of drag, for example, and the distinctions between butch and femme lesbian identities (Butler 1993; Butler 1999: 119–40, 163–90; Butler 2004: 57–101). And for Butler, like Sedgwick, these kinds of trouble can be made clearer or exacerbated by thinking of the identities thus troubled in the terms offered by a theory of performativity.

PERFORMATIVITY AND THE CONSTRUCTION OF IDENTITY

There is of course much more to Butler's dialogue with other feminist philosophers than this necessarily sketchy outline of her critique of the categories of identity suggests. What matters here, though, are the implications that can be drawn from her diagnosis of the trouble with gender, and the conceptual resources on which she draws in order to make good that diagnosis. The first significant implication of her position is this: if sex cannot justifiably be held up as an attribute of the merely natural body, if such a designation of the natural happens from *within* culture, then a different understanding of corporeality will have to be mobilised. Our bodies cannot be understood as standing outside culture, as the ground or origin of our social identities. But that doesn't mean that bodies should therefore be understood as inert or passive surfaces on which culture inscribes its meanings like an author writing on paper. That would merely reverse the terms, and therefore produce only a mirror-image of the rejected account of this relation – a mirror-image, in fact, that in characterising the body as passive, and culture as active, would be complicit with an age-old figuration of the passive body as female and the active, authorial principle that forms it as male. What is required is an account of this terrain that is able to get past the gendered polarity of natural bodies and cultural meanings, one that is able to rethink the complex relation between corporeality and identity. At the same time, though, this reworked sense of culture is being accorded a crucial role in the constitution of identity. Our identities are not given by nature or simply represented or expressed in culture: instead, culture is the process of identity formation, the way in which bodies and selves in all their differences are produced. So culture is a process, a kind of making, and we are what is made and remade through that process. Our activities and practices, in other words, are not expressions of some prior identity, or the things done by an agent that is what it is prior to its actions, but the very means by which we come to be what we are.

In order to articulate these challenging claims, Butler invokes the concept of performativity. The identity that we describe through the terms of gender is constituted through the performance of a set of *acts* that serve to forge us as gendered subjects, which is not at all the way that the customary understanding of gender roles would have it. As Butler says:

> Gender reality is performative which means, quite simply, that it is real only to the extent that it is performed. It seems fair to say that certain kinds of acts are usually interpreted as expressive of a gender core or identity, and that these acts either conform to an expected gender identity or contest that expectation in some way. That expectation, in turn, is based upon the perception of sex, where sex is understood to be the discrete and factic datum of primary sexual characteristics [i.e., the seemingly unarguable givenness of anatomical differences between male and female]. This implicit and popular theory of acts and gestures as expressive of gender suggests that gender itself is something prior to the various acts, postures, and gestures by which it is dramatized and known; indeed, gender appears to the popular imagination as a substantial core which might well be understood as the spiritual or psychological correlate of biological sex. If gender attributes, however, are not expressive but performative, then these attributes effectively constitute the identity they are said to express or reveal.
>
> (Butler 1990: 278–79)

In other words, the customary sense that the masculinity or femininity of what we *do* is expressive of what we *are*, and that what we are is a coherent unity of sex, gender and desire that can only properly happen one of two ways, is turned inside out by the invocation of performativity. Our gendered acts, the way we hold ourselves, the ways we speak, the spaces we occupy and how we occupy them, all in fact serve to create or bring about the multi-levelled self that these acts are so often taken merely to express or represent. As Butler says, in a much quoted passage:

> Gender ought not to be construed as a stable identity or locus of agency from which various acts follow; rather, gender is an identity tenuously constituted in time, instituted in an exterior space through a *stylized repetition of acts*. The effect of gender is produced through the stylization of the body and, hence, must be understood as the mundane way in which bodily gestures, movements, and styles of various kinds constitute the illusion of an abiding gendered self.
>
> (Butler 1999: 179)

These acts, then, as stylised and repeatable, taking place in the public world and reiterated through time, are *conventional*. There are conventional gestures, movements and styles which produce us as gendered, from the colours of the clothes we wear as babies, through the toys we play with as toddlers, the toilets we later use or the sports we are made to play at school, to the ways we learn to talk about ourselves as he or she; repeating these actions is how we come to be gendered, to take on a recognisable or conventional gender identity. Through the repetition of these recognised styles we come to *be* the gendered self we have learnt to perform. And these styles are not representations of an inner identity; nor are they the cultural expressions of an identity that is corporeally determined, since they are worked out through the stylisation of the body itself. If such performances are like Austinian performatives, in their 'pure' or declarative form, it is because they are constitutive: they create gender identity in being performed, bringing about the entity, the 'I', to which they refer. It is, though, vital to note here that Butler is *not* claiming that our *bodies* are thus constituted or constructed, as if they were somehow made out of culture. Rather, bodies compose or order themselves in this performative process, and we cannot know or 'experience' corporeality except through these compositional procedures. Yet there is more to this compositional process than this. It does not happen randomly: bodies compose themselves within the limits of a small range of viable roles. In particular, such acts produce us as men or women in a manner that reinforces the binary system of a 'heterosexual matrix': we can be only boys or girls, knights or princesses, have racing cars or flowers on our birthday cards, and princesses must wish one day to marry the knights who will eventually come to reciprocate their desire. Performances that do not serve to reinforce this law are repressed, mocked, denied recognition: small girls who don't like dolls will learn to play properly; knights will not grow up to marry other knights.

THE POWER OF GENDER NORMS

Now, this is clearly a use of the concept of performativity that expands its frame of reference. Yet it is also surprisingly faithful to some of the implications of the Austinian performative that we have traced in preceding chapters. For a start, Butler's strategy mimics Austin's polemical engagements to some degree: she takes over his initial distinction between performative and constative, a distinction that served the strategic function of disputing positivist accounts of language as primarily descriptive, in order to displace accounts of gender acts that might see them as merely descriptive of an underlying or determining ground or essence. Furthermore, while Butler's emphasis on acts stresses that these are not to be thought of only or primarily as linguistic, Austin's own sense of how illocutionary force might be manifested also made room for gesture, ritual and other non-discursive sets of sense-making conventions: indeed, as Searle later showed, it could be extended to a consideration of the general structure of both formal and informal social institutions. And if we understand the conventional nature of the speech act as that which underpins its capacity to constitute an event in the world, then Butler's assertion that such acts precede or help to create their actors, or that such actors can become actors only in performing those acts that the culture makes possible, looks somewhat similar. Indeed, at one point in *Gender Trouble* Butler even speaks of the performance of gender as the product of a 'tacit collective agreement' (Butler 1999: 178; see also Butler 1990: 273), thus recalling the imagery of the implicit contract that has stalked prior attempts to define the role of conventions in the functioning of the speech act.

Nonetheless, there are some very important differences. For ordinary language philosophy, as we have seen, the conventionality of the speech situation is part of the 'necessary conditions of the shared world'. The normativity of any speech act registers its implicit invocation of criteria that open it to assessment as valid or otherwise. The appeal to the ordinary is the demand that such pragmatic normativity be recognised as at work in all language, as inseparable from its functioning. Yet if our speaking must invoke norms in this way, Austin is silent on their force or extent, and on the political character and moral worth of particular norms or of such normativity in general. For him, it is seemingly enough to call philosophy back to this way of recognising the everyday communal dimension of linguistic life; for Cavell after him, though, as we saw in chapter two, the acknowledgement of this way of sharing a world does suggest new openings for political and ethical thought. Butler's account of the norms of gender, however, depends on radically different presuppositions. The performative norm for Butler is a form of compulsion, and the composition of the body itself an exercise in confining it within a limit. Bodies are *normalised*, and they suffer under the weight of the conventions that they are thus brought to repeat. Far from registering a fragile mutuality, overlooked by the philosophical and political discourses that claim to map the world, normativity marks out a social realm inhabited by both relatively successfully gendered subjects and the abjected, excluded or penalised bodies of those who define the limits of the norm by falling outside it.

Crucial to Butler's account of the normativity of the performative, then, is an understanding of the force and power that characterise the social relations among speaking bodies. The force inhabiting the speech situation for her cannot be, as it is for Austin when he speaks of illocutionary force, simply a matter of validity. Her main influence here is in fact the theory of modern sexuality presented by the French philosopher Michel Foucault, a theory in which power itself was delineated in a strikingly original way. For Foucault, force was certainly not a matter of criterial validity, but nor should it be defined as primarily a matter of law or government, its operations understood as the prohibition or containment of energies and possibilities arising from other sources, as a repressive state apparatus, say, might clamp down on the carnivalesque energies of an unruly populace. In fact, the various institutions and discourses that constitute the social are in Foucault's analyses instances of a productive or positive mode of power, and actually serve to constitute that which they merely claim to know (see especially Foucault 1979, 1977 and 1980). Thus, for instance, the modern era witnesses the development of medical and other discourses that set out such categories of human identity as sexuality, including the classification or definition of sexual types. One of the ways these kinds of seemingly disinterested, scientific projects justify themselves is by establishing an understanding of sexuality as an element in the fixed essence of what it is to be human, and then setting out to uncover or reveal the 'truth' of this essence. Such projects do not proceed only by discursive means, though, since they are forged through institutions such as universities, hospitals and other agencies that emerge as part of the same process, and that make practical interventions into the everyday embodied lives of those they set out to classify and organise.

That such kinds of power are positive, however, does not mean that they are in any sense necessarily benign or simply transparent. In Foucault's analyses, such discourses tend towards the regulation or normalisation of their subjects; thus, the classification of sexualities coincides with the identification of a 'normal' or 'proper' sexuality and attempts both to treat and prevent manifestations that are held to fall beyond it. Our identities, therefore, are the product of these various processes of discipline and organisation, of regulation and cultivation, to which we are subject. The mobility or fluidity in this model stems from the claim that although power is everywhere, it does not stem from a single source or centre. In fact, there is no such thing as 'power' in the singular: there is only a 'multiplicity of force relations' (Foucault 1979: 92). Furthermore, that power here is conceived as a *relation* of force means that it is not just travelling outwards from a single source, working itself out on some passive or inert object. Different discourses or institutions may well be at odds with each other; the elaboration of a set of norms or disciplinary procedures may well have consequences which exceed the workings of the procedure in question. Thus, in Foucault's often cited but historically questionable example, the classification and regulation of the category of 'homosexual' in the mid- to late nineteenth century did not just serve to produce a set of compliant, self-proclaimed inverts or perverts. Instead, taken up in other discourses and institutional contexts, the category of 'homosexuality' became the resource for a demand for political and legal recognition on the part of those thus classified, even as it also perpetuated the particular way of thinking about the nature of 'sexuality' and its place in human identity that had underpinned the original discourse (Foucault 1979: 100–102). Our identities, therefore, although they are forged and recognised through the regulatory and classificatory work of the various discourses and institutions in which they are formulated and practised, are not necessarily singular or simple.

POLITICS AND PERFORMATIVITY

Foucault is far from being the only resource that Butler uses in her account of the social production of identity: in fact, she is very interested in the psychoanalytic accounts of such production in the work of Sigmund Freud and Jacques Lacan, and in her 1997 book *The Psychic Life of Power* she seeks to draw the psychoanalytic and Foucauldian accounts closer together. However, it is Foucault's account of sexuality as the normalising work of power that does much to condition her conception of gender performativity. While Foucault does not necessarily count power as repressive, his narrative of its creativity, of the composing and ordering of subjects, is often and not unreasonably read as a political challenge to the very processes he documents. In particular, it is a challenge to the thinking of sex as a human essence that we could and should seek disinterestedly to know. For Butler, too, the norms of gender that form us are profoundly troubling, and the model of identity that is called upon to justify their normalising work is as much a focus for her critical attentions as the modern category of sexuality is for Foucault. For this reason, Butler's understanding of the conventionality of the performative differs from that of previous theories.

For all that Butler criticises the regulatory work of gender performatives, though, she also sees performativity as offering one of the best chances for opposing that work. The force she associates with the performative is partly a normalising power that constitutes by exclusion: in producing the normal, it also produces the abnormal, that which falls outside the realm of a 'proper' identity. A heterosexual norm is therefore haunted by the non-heterosexual that it must imagine in order to be what it is. So, for Butler, there always remains a chance within the performativity of identity for dissonant or disruptive gestures by that which such performativity produces as its outside. She theorises this chance in more than one way. Sometimes the production of stable identities is understood as an impossible project, as a work of identification that is constitutively incapable of being completed:

> The practice by which gendering occurs, the embodying of norms, is a compulsory practice, a forcible production, but not for that reason

> fully determining. To the extent that gender is an assignment, it is an assignment which is never quite carried out according to expectation, whose addressee never quite inhabits the ideal s/he is compelled to approximate.
>
> (Butler 1993: 231)

This position is argued most clearly from a psychoanalytic standpoint, and understood in terms of the complex relations between psychic imperatives that do not all pull in the same direction (see Butler 1993: 93–119; Butler 1999: 73–91). But she also links these analyses to an emphasis on the repetitive structure of performatives: precisely because the ideal is never accomplished, it must always be attempted again. This focus on repetition further permits the suggestion that the norms thus repeated and recited themselves become vulnerable in their repetition. They are in the end nothing but their repetition, they exist as norms only on that temporal basis, and they do not and cannot programme or determine everything that is possible. They are not, therefore, a law that we are simply condemned to obey; they *become* law-like only through being repeated, re-enacted, and the spell could be broken. Thus, for Butler, the chance for a political intervention occurs because the work of gendering is vulnerable in what she calls its 'iterability' or its 'citationality'.

These terms are of course borrowed from Derrida. Butler does not, however, take over the Derridean account of iterability wholesale; in fact, as we shall see, she finds it wanting as an account of the political possibilities of the performative. But she does follow his use of citationality to some extent. In particular she adapts for her purposes Derrida's deconstruction of the distinction between serious and non-serious speech acts, finding in his assertion that the former could not succeed without participating in the citationality attributed to the latter a resource for unsettling attempts to read the 'serious' performance of gender itself as properly expressive of an underlying identity. In this way of thinking, there would be an obvious distinction between the expressive way in which a 'real' or 'natural' woman 'performs' her femininity, and the mere hollow mimicry of a drag queen or a pantomime dame. Yet for Butler, as I noted above, this kind of natural expressiveness is not what it seems: it is in fact just an illusory *effect* of the repeated performance of the acts of gender, acts that 'congeal over time

to produce the appearance of substance, of a natural sort of being'
(Butler 1999: 43–44). As she puts it elsewhere, iterability or citationality is the dissimulatory process 'by which the subject who "cites" the
performative is temporarily produced as the belated and fictive origin of
the performative itself' (Butler 1997a: 49). This dissimulation or fiction
is a crucial element in the compulsory and compulsive performance of
gender, as the citational nature of the acts is denied and concealed.
Gender is thus a groundless performance, a kind of fiction, that presents
itself otherwise in *appearing* to proceed from a prior ground or origin.
Our gendered behaviour seems to be an aspect of a natural or given
identity, but that identity is itself a product of the performative process.
So the politics of gender performativity as Butler sees it will consist in
exposing this process to view, revealing the pervasive performativity
that our standard accounts of identity fail to see.

THE ENACTMENT OF CRITIQUE

Such critique, though, does not just take the form of a theoretical intervention. In fact, in both *Gender Trouble* and *Bodies That Matter*, Butler
dwells on ways in which the performance of gender might itself be not
the participation in the normalising, dissimulating work of power, but
instead a kind of enacted critique. Her prime instance of this is the drag
act performed as part of a gay culture. Drawing on the work of the
anthropologist Esther Newton, she argues that drag in these contexts
has the potential to break up the illusory coherence, the apparent naturalness, of identity that is presumed to underlie the performance of gendered acts. Drag acts in these contexts, Newton argues, make two
simultaneous but incompatible claims, both of which invert the normal
order of gendered identity. On the one hand, the donning of drag
demonstrates that the performer's outside appearance – clothes, posture,
intonation – is feminine, but that the inside, the body, is masculine; on
the other hand, and at the same time, drag suggests that the body considered as outside is masculine, but the inner self, paradoxically
unveiled by the clothes, is feminine (Newton 1972: 103, cited in Butler
1999: 174). The peculiar pressure exerted on the thinking of a natural
or coherent gender identity here comes from the simultaneity of these
two moments: not only does drag combine apparently incompatible
masculinity and femininity, it also manages to undo the assumption

that there is any means to make a clear judgement about which gender performance here is authentic or real. Challenging the expressive model that would offer a basis for discriminating between 'real' or 'authentic' performances of gender and the 'unreal' or 'fake', the drag act thus performs the critical insight that all gender acts are equally, if variously, citational. To the extent that everyone's gender is therefore fabricated, rather than expressed, then everyone is in some kind of drag. If that is the case, then the spurious naturalisation of identity that works through the compulsory normalisation of gender can be *shown* to be spurious. What had looked like a given or necessary order of gender propriety stands revealed as merely contingent. And drag can also make a further, related kind of trouble, if we take into account Butler's claim that gender acts are compulsively repeated because they never quite manage to live up to the ideal demanded. A man in drag is understood to be imitating a femininity he does not actually embody; but if no performance can ever live up to femininity, then no one can possess it, and all gender acts are an imitation of an unreachable ideal. In this way, then, 'drag imitates the imitative structure of gender'; in so doing, it is 'revealing gender itself to be an imitation', a copy, a citation of an 'original' that does not exist (Butler 1997b: 145).

Drag is far from alone in offering the possibility of this kind of critique. What coherent assemblage of sex, gender and sexuality could the intersex individual be expressing, for example, when s/he performs either masculine or feminine gender roles? Can such an individual be either convincingly assimiliated into the normal dualism of heterosexuality, or convincingly excluded as homosexual? What has happened to the unchangeable givenness of bodily sex when the body in question is transsexual? The playing out of masculinity and femininity in the lesbian context of butch and femme identities, such that it can make sense for a femme to say that 'she likes her boys to be girls', also undoes the coherence of presumed identity in a similar fashion (Butler 1999: 156). All these can serve as instances in which the category of identity itself, as Butler hoped, could be rendered problematic, because they are all instances in which a presumed coherence is undone, shown to be illusory. The concealed contingency of identity is thus revealed as this coherence is unsettled; the performativity that establishes the norm turns back to challenge it. So performativity works both ways:

Performativity describes this relation of being implicated in that which one opposes, this turning of power against itself to produce alternative modalities of power, to establish a kind of political contestation that is not a 'pure' opposition, a 'transcendence' of contemporary relations of power, but a difficult labor of forging a future from resources inevitably impure.

(Butler 1993: 241)

In both *Gender Trouble* and *Bodies that Matter*, Butler describes this kind of enacted critique as a process of 'resignification'. Acts repeat; but they can repeat differently. Thus, gender acts can be turned towards undermining their organising norms even as they 'cite' them, since 'the task is not whether to repeat, but how to repeat or, indeed, to repeat and, through a radical proliferation of gender, to displace the very gender norms that enable the repetition itself' (Butler 1999: 189).

In the context of her early work, this strategy of subversive resignification serves the purpose of exposing the illusion that gendered acts, and therefore gender itself, are stable components in a coherent and necessary order of identity. Subsequently, however, Butler has extended the reach of this term to cover other instances of such 'repeating differently'. She has, for example, used it to describe the act of Rosa Parks, the American civil rights activist who in 1955 remained seated on a bus in Montgomery, Alabama when white passengers were standing, even though the regulations demanded that a black person occupying that seat should give it up in such circumstances (Butler 1997a: 147). Black 'voters' arriving at the polling station during elections in apartheid South Africa, even though they had no legal right to vote, also exemplified this kind of resignification for Butler; the appropriation of the insulting name 'queer' by gay activists and theorists is a further, well known instance (see Butler 2004: 223–24). In all of these cases a twist is given to the normal act in its 'deviant' repetition. Mis-performing the acts proper to whites presents a challenge to the norms that secure white privilege and dominance, a challenge that in Rosa Parks' case was to have wide-ranging consequences for the future of racial segregation in the American South; similarly, 'citing' a term like 'queer' beyond and against its function as insult challenges its power to hurt and stigmatise. Here, resignification is less clearly a means of exposing illusory claims to naturalness, as if the revelation of an act's citationality were enough to make the critical intervention stick. It is instead the term for a more generalised form of political work, and it is extended in this direction by Butler as part of her intervention into heated legal and philosophical debates around pornography and 'hate speech' that loomed large in the political landscape of the United States during the early 1990s.

'HATE SPEECH' IN LEGAL THEORY

The essays gathered in *Excitable Speech* set out the substance of Butler's intervention into these debates. In this book she makes much more explicit use of Austin's thinking on the performative than is the case in her earlier work on gender and identity; indeed, as she has admitted, her dealings with Austin in that earlier work were conducted only through her reading of Derrida (Bell 1999: 164–65). Here, too, she offers a more thoroughgoing engagement with Derrida's deconstruction of Austin, an engagement that also clarifies the extent of her distance from Derrida's work. It is here that theories of performativity *per se* are addressed, and where her own claims for the broad political promise of performative 'resignification' are most thoroughly developed. This is possible in the context of legal controversies around the social functioning and powers of speech because such debates feature arguments that can themselves be cast in Austinian or speech act theoretical terms. Butler's attention is thus drawn to the contrasting ways in which judges, legislators and theorists seek to make sense of speech as a kind of social action, and her conception of performativity is offered as a critical counterweight to these understandings.

In following this line, Butler focuses particularly on a United States Supreme Court judgement in 1992 concerning the nature of the action undertaken by a white boy from St Paul, Minnesota in burning a cross in front of a black family's home. Such an act, recalling one of the ritual practices of the racist Ku Klux Klan, might be considered a form of threatening behaviour, or 'disorderly conduct', as a St Paul city ordinance forbidding such actions had put it. To 'speak' in this way was to do something, and specifically to do something injurious to someone else: the city ordinance assumed an easy equation here between speech and conduct. Yet the Supreme Court instead argued that the burning cross was the expression of a viewpoint, the exercise of free speech, and as such was protected under the First Amendment of the Constitution. In so doing, they drew a line between speech and conduct, suggesting that a burning cross was no more than an admittedly unpleasant contribution to a separable realm of legitimate public discussion, the 'free marketplace of ideas' (Butler 1997a: 53). As Butler suggests, this interpretation is one that sees language as essentially constative, a realm of descriptions at one remove from the 'real' world of actions, while the St Paul city ordinance is more clearly alert to the pragmatic dimension of such speech (Butler 1997a: 56). Adopting this Austinian terminology, though, produces a further question. How is the pragmatic dimension of utterance to be understood here? We could approach a speech act such as this in terms of its *perlocutionary* force, attempting to trace the effects that it contingently produces as a *consequence* of its utterance. So we could consider it as injurious in terms of the fear that such a racist act causes in those confronted with it, or perhaps note the damaging effects on community relations more broadly. Could we, though, also speak of such an act as having illocutionary force?

In one, purely Austinian sense, we clearly could. Such an act could well meet the criteria for a threat, the inverse of a promise. By the same token, the calling of someone 'queer' might be classified as an insult, another recognisably illocutionary act. Butler, though, finds herself considering a rather different set of arguments for the performativity of such 'hate speech', arguments that are more clearly related to her own discussions of the constitution of identity. As we have seen, for Butler identity is produced through the repetition of imitative or citational acts: the subject, the speaker or 'doer', is thus the creation of the doing, a creation dissimulated as the deed's origin. This she takes to be the opposite of the Austinian outline of the speech act, though it is much more securely opposed to the account given by Searle. In such an account the 'serious' or proper act is animated or inhabited by the intention of an agent, a speaker who really is, therefore, the origin of the deed. Now, the illocutionary force of hate speech might be understood as related to an agent or subject in this way. It could also be comprehended as the production of a subject, in the sense that its speaker is forged or formed through the citation of these kinds of utterances. Racism, then, need not be understood as primarily a state of mind that can then sometimes break out into speech or violence, and it would not be open to the speakers of racist words to exculpate themselves by complaining that although they said the wrong thing, yet they harboured not a racist bone in their bodies. Instead, their identity as racist would be constituted through their reiteration of hate speech.

PERFORMATIVITY AND INTERPELLATION

There is, though, a third possibility that Butler now has to consider, since it has been asserted as one of the ways in which hate speech performs its damaging work. It can be claimed that those *named* or *identified* by such threats and insults, those who are the addressees of such utterances, are thereby produced as injured parties. This 'performative' scene, as Butler argues, owes more to the Marxist philosopher Louis Althusser than it does to speech act theory (Butler 1997a: 24–34). According to Althusser, the subject is produced through a process he called 'interpellation', in which she or he is 'hailed' or addressed by a powerful ideology (see Althusser 1971). Responding to the address, as one might turn and respond to a shouted 'hey you', the subject takes on the identity of the 'you' thus hailed. This is a view that in a more sophisticated version has underpinned the efforts of the feminist legal theorist, Catherine Mackinnon, to justify legislation prohibiting pornography. The speech acts of porn have effects that are more than perlocutionary, more than a matter of hurtful consequences: porn instead directly harms and degrades not only the women who are abused in its production, but also damages all women in interpellating 'woman' as an object, subordinated and silenced (Mackinnon 1993). As Butler says,

> According to this illocutionary model, hate speech *constitutes* its addressee at the moment of its utterance; it does not describe an injury or produce one as a consequence; it is, in the very speaking of such speech, the performance of the injury itself, where the injury is understood as social subordination.
>
> (Butler 1997a: 18)

Although this model echoes Butler's own investment in and adaptation of the concept of performativity, she also wishes to measure her distance from it. In particular, she is concerned that the kind of injurious address imagined by Mackinnon is presented as overwhelmingly *effective*:

I wish to question for the moment the presumption that hate speech always works, not to minimize the pain that is suffered as a consequence of hate speech, but to leave open the possibility that its failure is the condition of a critical response. . . . Even if hate speech works to constitute a subject through discursive means, is that constitution necessarily final and effective? Is there a possibility of disrupting and subverting the effects produced by such speech, a faultline that leads to the undoing of this process of discursive constitution? What kind of power is *attributed to* speech such that speech is figured as having the power to constitute the subject with such success?

(Butler 1997a: 19)

In other words, where is the possibility for resistance in the scene of address that Mackinnon presents? To ask again the Foucauldian question posed earlier: can this kind of performativity do no more than perpetuate or reiterate domination? Is there anything that might give an oppositional politics its chance?

As we might by now expect, Butler wants to insist that there is. The motivation for her insistence on such a possibility is a profound ambivalence regarding the turn to law and censorship that Mackinnon and others have urged. Certainly, if sexist, racist and homophobic discourse is as remorselessly constitutive as has been implied, then state prohibitions might seem to be the only way in which such performativity could be interrupted or arrested. As Butler points out, however, such prohibitions can look uncomfortably similar to the kinds of disciplinary and repressive measures urged against 'deviant' or 'abnormal' genders and sexualities. The 'graphic self-representation' of a gay artist, for example, might well find itself subject to a law against the production and distribution of pornographic imagery, as might the 'explicit sexual education' needed to combat sexually transmitted diseases such as AIDS (Butler 1997a: 22). So in place of this perhaps dangerous resort to legislation, she asserts the scope for other kinds of response to the social subordination sought, enacted or confirmed by hate speech. But this means that in place of the frighteningly 'mechanical and predictable' performativity that she finds in the models of Mackinnon and others (Butler 1997a: 19), she must present an alternative account of how the performative works.

RESIGNIFICATION AND THE BODY

Crucial to this is the concept of resignification developed in her earlier work. Hate speech can only have its constitutive power on account of its iterability; but this iterability itself ensures that every repetition is the occasion of an irreducible difference. The repetition of injurious words is traumatic, in the sense of repeating or reliving the injury, but it is also the opportunity for 'reverse citation', for turning or reworking the force of the damaging word. This, for example, was precisely what happened to 'queer'; it is also what has been attempted with terms such as 'nigger'. Such attempts at reversal have not always been recognised as successful: Butler quotes a claim that 'words such as "nigger" and "spick" are badges of degradation even when used between friends: *these words have no other connotation*' (Butler 1997a: 100). She points out, though, that this claim is necessarily qualified or contradicted even as it is made. When its author quoted or cited those words, he was not simply using them. The fact that they *could* be quoted or cited is evidence enough for the difference that iterability necessarily makes possible:

> Even if we concede – as I think we must – ... that it is difficult to utter those words or, indeed, to write them here, because they unwittingly recirculate that degradation, it does not follow that such words can have no other connotation. Indeed, their repetition is necessary (in court, as testimony; in psychoanalysis, as traumatic emblems; in aesthetic modes, as a cultural working-through) in order to enter them as objects of another discourse. Paradoxically, their status as 'act' is precisely what undermines the claim that they evidence and actualize the degradation that they intend. As acts, these words ... become a kind of linguistic display that does not overcome their degrading meanings, but that reproduces them as public text and that, in being reproduced, displays them as reproducible and resignifiable terms. The possibility of decontextualizing and recontextualizing such terms through radical acts of public misappropriation constitutes the basis of an ironic hopefulness that the conventional relation between word and wound might become tenuous and even broken over time.
>
> (Butler 1997a: 100)

There is, then, hope, even if only ironic hope; and where there is hope, then there can also be politics.

The theoretical grounds for this hope would appear to be Derridean. Butler's claim here seems to be underpinned by Derrida's assertion that all language necessarily depends on a citationality that allows the repetition of the same only on the condition of a necessary difference. Yet as Butler goes on to outline the basis on which her claims for resignification can be justified she argues that there are limitations in Derrida's approach. Firstly, she acknowledges the worth of the concept of iterability in indicating the reason why structures of social and discursive authority or legitimacy should not be seen as static. The French sociologist Pierre Bourdieu criticised Austin for not recognising that the force of utterance derives from forms of social domination that are not linguistic; such a critique, though, ends up implying that language, if it is a conventional system, is therefore inert, a mere instrument for the extra-linguistic social forces that mobilise it (Bourdieu 1991: 107–16; Butler 1997a: 146–47). What Derrida rightly preserves is the sense that some kind of force inheres in conventional structures on account of their conventionality. As we saw in chapters four and five, Derrida also argued that the iterability that underlies the possibility of a system of conventions is at the same time the means by which things happen otherwise, the opportunity for ' "literatures" or "revolutions" that as yet have no model', as he puts it in *Limited Inc* (Derrida 1988: 100). There can be no conventionality that is simply 'mechanical' or 'predictable', no machine of this sort that is not in some way an exploding machine.

Yet Butler does not in fact think that this insight could itself offer enough of a basis for a theory of resignification. For a start, she takes the exposition of iterability to be a way of defining the force of the performative *itself*: 'The force of the performative,' Butler suggests, 'is thus not inherited from prior usage, but issues forth precisely from its break with any and all prior usage. That break, that force of rupture, is the force of the performative' (Butler 1997a: 148). And because iterability is everywhere in any system of marks, any linguistic structure, this same kind of force is also everywhere. Butler thus argues that the Derridean version of iterability, the iterability of the mark *per se*, is overly formal: in positing iterability as a *structural* feature of *all* marks, and therefore of all conventional systems or institutions, this account is too abstract, too universal, to support the kind of analysis of performativity that Butler wants to pursue. 'Derrida,' she says, 'appears to install the break as a structurally necessary feature of every utterance and every codifiable written mark, thus paralyzing the social analysis of forceful utterance' (Butler 1997a: 150). In other words, deconstruction is too formal a resource for making sense of how performativity works through bodies as a mode of interpellation. Butler wants to be able to focus on what she calls 'social iterability', the forces through which the body is stylised and composed in 'embodied rituals of everydayness' (Butler 1997a: 150, 152). This would be a notion of the social that includes language, but cannot be captured by the kind of purely linguistic, and overly general, model of performative force that she here takes Derrida to be offering.

The kind of performativity that Butler is interested in, then, works itself out through the body: 'social conventions' can be seen as 'animating the bodies which, in turn, reproduce and ritualize those conventions as practices'; the force of performativity is that of 'a citational chain lived and believed at the level of the body' (Butler 1997a: 155). How, though, can the chance of resignification now be comprehended? How can it be possible, if not on the structural basis Derrida set out? Here, too, Butler invokes the force of corporeality itself. 'The body,' she suggests, 'is not simply a sedimentation of speech acts by which it has been constituted. If that constitution fails, a resistance meets interpellation at the moment it exerts its demand' (Butler 1997a: 155). Why, though, on this account, should interpellation fail? To answer this, Butler turns to the work of the American literary critic Shoshana Felman, whose distinctive engagement with Austin's thinking on the performative was first published in French in 1980, then translated into English and issued under the title *The Literary Speech Act* three years later. The book's concerns are more clearly revealed by the title of the French edition, restored when the translation was reissued two decades later as *The Scandal of the Speaking Body* (Felman 2002). What Butler takes from Felman's account, as she says in her Afterword to the 2002 edition, is the emphasis on the consequences of apprehending the performative as corporeal (Butler 2002: 113). Felman's insight, the 'scandal' that she explores, is that the speaking body is both the condition for any possible performative utterance, and the occasion for an excess of 'saying' over what is said:

> For Felman, the body that speaks is a scandal . . . because the bodily action of speech is not predictable in any mechanical way. That the

speech act is a bodily act does not mean that the body is fully present in its speech ... Speech is bodily, but the body exceeds the speech it occasions; and speech remains irreducible to the bodily means of its enunciation.

(Butler 1997a: 155–56)

Thus, the body actually *interferes* with the process of sedimentation, of composition or ordering through repetition, that it has to undergo. It is not just the predictable product of that process of identity formation or subjection, and the promise of resignification can be apprehended once the power or agency of corporeality itself is considered. In this way, Butler seeks to locate the political opportunities of the performative in a theory of social iterability that neither neglects the body nor, as a consequence, finds itself unable to give a proper account of the particular interplay of constitutive domination and challenging resistance that takes place through its social life:

In such bodily productions resides the sedimented history of the performative, the ways in which sedimented usage comes to compose, without determining, the cultural sense of the body, and how the body comes to disorient that cultural sense in the moment of expropriating the discursive means of its own production. The appropriation of such norms to oppose their historically sedimented effect constitutes the insurrectionary moment of that history, the moment that founds a future through a break with that past.

(Butler 1997a: 159)

WHAT IS THE FORCE OF THE PERFORMATIVE?

In recasting iterability in this way, Butler claims that she has revealed 'the political promise of the performative', and in so doing opened up 'an unanticipated political future for deconstructive thinking' (Butler 1997a: 161). Her sense that the deconstructive analysis, for all its strengths, cannot attend effectively to the ways in which performativity works as a social force finds an echo in Eve Kosofsky Sedgwick's warning that a theory of performativity 'needn't and shouldn't have the effect of hiving off a depersonalized understanding of performative force from a psychologized and spatialized understanding of affective force'

(Sedgwick 2003: 90). Sedgwick, though, also suggests that Butler's formulations are themselves cast too generally: her own project of 'attending to the textures and effects of particular bits of language' thus 'requires a step to the side of anti-essentialism', the larger claims about the relation between doing and being that inform Butler's thinking about performativity (Sedgwick 2003: 6). This recasting of deconstruction, though, also raises a few questions. It is impelled by Butler's dissatisfaction with the suggestion that the 'breaking force' of a generalised iterability is identical with the force of the performative, a suggestion that she attributes to Derrida. This, though, is not quite right. As we saw in previous chapters, Derrida does indeed suggest that without iterability no performative could have force: if iterability is indeed in one of its moments a condition of the possibility of any successful or valid performative, as Derrida argues, then the shifting between contexts of which an iterable mark is necessarily capable must underpin the capacity of the performative to do its work, to have any illocutionary force. But this observation is not an assertion that these forces are *one and the same*. Derrida does not in fact *elide* the 'breaking force' of iterability and the illocutionary force of the performative. For him, the latter is what it is for Austin, the invocation of a normative validity implicit in all utterances. Iterability makes both possible and vulnerable the *sameness* of a mark in two or more contexts, a sameness without which it would make no sense whatsoever to talk of conventions, rules or norms. But the force of the performative for Derrida is still a matter of accordance with such norms: this underpins an increasing suspicion of the concept of performativity in his pursuit of a politics and ethics more thoroughly attentive to the difference of the unanticipated other, the surprising 'event'. 'Wherever there is the performative, whatever the form of communication', he asserts, 'there is a context of legitimate, legitimizing, or legitimized convention' (Derrida 2000: 467). The breaking force of iterability, in other words, does not supplant the appeal to norms as the determinant of performative force. Rather, it complicates or supplements it, ensuring that illocutionary or performative force can never simply be accounted for by such an appeal.

This difference suggests in turn a somewhat different approach to the relations between performativity and linguistic normativity. Derrida portrayed his engagement with speech act theory, as I noted in chapter five, as a way of allowing the law-enforcement or policing role of such a theory to come out into the open. Butler's own account of performatives portrays them as necessarily operating through the compulsory but dissimulated repetition of social norms that serve to circumscribe the field of who can count as fully human (see Butler 2004: 206, 220–22). Both of them seek to mark the possibility of resistance to this kind of force. For Derrida, this is important as a way of formulating a space for an ethical or political responsibility that does not simply seek to ground itself in a system of rules; for Butler, what matters is a political resistance to the process by which those whom the norms exclude are condemned to 'live' impossible lives. Performativity, for her, is therefore both the often traumatic force of normalisation and that which resists it.

What perhaps is lost in both these approaches, though, is the sense of the *weakness* of normativity as it appears in the appeal to ordinary language made by Austin and Cavell, the vulnerability of responsibilities and commitments that are never simply impersonal or transcendent or law-like in this fashion, even as they are not simply the voluntary acts of sovereign subjects. What such an emphasis also disregards is the way in which such an appeal opposes itself to the ever-vigorous search for a certainty or a ground beyond the facts of our lives together. The attention to felicity conditions in Austin's conception of illocutionary force need not therefore be an appeal to the unarguable self-evidence of a dogmatic foundation. If a speech act is, as Cavell puts it, 'an offer of participation in the order of law' (Cavell 2005: 185), then that law need not be one that is simply oppressive or imposed, one where participation is both compulsory and yet only possible on iniquitous terms. Butler's sense of the norms that structure society has little room for this other picture of normativity, since she takes as her starting point the recognition that psycho-social suffering or trauma necessarily accompanies such structuring.

In the end, though, she does acknowledge that the kind of political drama of domination and resistance her thinking of performativity imagines will not be enough. The resignification of a norm, for example, will not of itself guarantee that this resistant act will be either good or progressive. After all, the Nazis resignified a few norms as part of their seizure of power in the Germany of the 1930s (Butler 2004: 224). The advocacy of this kind of resistance, then, will need to be accompanied by a working out of questions of right or value, and this will be precisely a process of attending to norms of some kind. Such norms 'have to be derived from a radical democratic theory and practice', a form of democracy that allows its participants 'to live a life politically, in relation to power, in relation to others, in the act of assuming responsibility for a collective future' (Butler 2004: 224, 226). But where, in the world that Butler describes, are we to find resources for such a practice? The account of social norms or commitments that she presents in theorising performativity might appear to offer little prospect for such a future, which is perhaps why her subsequent work has addressed the possibility of non-normalising family and social relations, and has turned more recently to focus on the question of how the ethical demand for responsibility and obligation might be shown to be compatible with her account of subject formation (see Butler 2000; 2005). This might seem to suggest that the concept of performativity needs to be transcended in order to rescue normativity for democratic and ethical purposes. As we saw in chapter two, though, the thinking of the performative has all along opened onto political and ethical prospects beyond a partnership of normalisation and resistance.

7

PERFORMATIVITY AND PERFORMANCE THEORY

When we enter whatever theatre our lives allow us, we have already learned how strange and many-layered everyday life is, how extraordinary the ordinary.

(Turner 1982: 122)

In recent years the concept of performativity has become a prominent feature in the broader academic field of performance studies. This discipline is itself a fairly recent invention: only in the last two decades or so has it achieved the institutional status and paraphernalia of an established area of study. Performance studies is to some degree an extension of theatre studies, a recognition that the genres of performance worthy of academic attention are neither limited to what we usually call drama nor constrained within the space of the stage. Arts such as dance, music and story-telling, as well as a wide variety of ceremonies, rituals and games, have all therefore been the focus for an attention that focuses on their performance dimension. Unsurprisingly, this investigation has both drawn on and helped to foster a strand of lively theoretical work. A range of intellectual frameworks from disciplines including anthropology, sociology, philosophy and literary studies have all furnished resources for the construction of a body of performance theory that is capable both of justifying and challenging this attention to a broadly conceived range of performances.

BUTLER AND PERFORMANCE THEORY

'Performative' is one of the most prominent terms in this new theoretical vocabulary. It has not necessarily been borrowed from Austin, though, nor from the intertwined traditions developed in response to his work; or if it has been thus borrowed, it is the term rather than the concept that has been transplanted. Whereas for Austin 'performative' could be both a noun or an adjective, and its meaning was specialised and technical, in performance theory it has been used adjectivally and quite generally to denote the performance aspect of any object or practice under consideration. Thus, for example, to address culture as 'performative' would be simply to examine it as some kind of performance, without the specific implications that would follow from an invocation of the line of thought first developed distinctively by Austin. 'Performativity' would therefore mean only the rather general quality something might have by virtue of being a performance. Yet in the wake of Judith Butler's work, in particular, what we might call Austinian performativity looms rather large in performance theory, and the narrative of his own thinking and its adaptation by Derrida and Butler has itself become a prominent part of the latter's intellectual heritage. This doubled history of the term is sometimes the source of problems, though, since neither of these two usages has yet managed to displace or entirely accommodate itself to the other. Their relation is instead best described as *asymptotic*: an ever-closer proximity without a final, resolving convergence. In this chapter, we will see how shared concerns and problems might draw performance theory and Austinian performativity together; in doing so, we should also be able to see possible differences that such proximity might otherwise cause us to overlook.

It is ironic, in fact, that Butler should be the thinker most often credited with effecting the union of this line of thinking about performativity and performance theory. As we saw in the last chapter, she came late to Austin, and then somewhat grudgingly, seeing his work largely through the lenses provided by Derrida and of little value in itself (Bell 1999: 164). Her own version of the performative is also a substantial rewriting of the Derridean account and departs somewhat from his concerns. Interestingly enough, an essay published in the same year as *Gender Trouble*, repeatedly referenced, taught and anthologised in performance studies in subsequent years, anchors its account of the performativity of gender not in Austin nor in Derrida but in the works of prominent performance theorists such as the Scottish anthropologist Victor Turner (see Butler 1990: 277–78), though this anchorage is not apparent in *Gender Trouble* itself. It is only in her subsequent books that the Austinian and Derridean heritage with which she is more commonly associated comes increasingly into view.

Butler's thinking, then, is already indebted to performance theory at its origin, before such theory reciprocated by borrowing from her analyses; for this reason, Butler's version of the concept is itself marked by the double history of performativity that is evident in performance theory more generally. In speaking of gender as an act, she draws on the dramatic or theatrical senses of 'act' in order to pursue her case, understanding the 'doing' of gender as the 'dramatization' of the body, a matter of 'ritualized, public performance' (Butler 1990: 272 and 277). More centrally, the nature of her critique of gender identity makes a resort to concepts of theatrical performance necessary. As we have seen, Butler takes aim at a particular *ontological* understanding of gender, one that sees identity as essence. It is to be found in the substance of a body or the self-sameness of a subject existing prior to and as the origin of the deeds that express it. In this view, one *is* a woman, and being a woman, one *does* womanly things. Clothes, gestures, styles are therefore all merely *expressive* of one's given gender identity. Confronting this dominant gender ontology, Butler explores the potential of an enacted critique that could reveal it for the dissimulation she claims it to be. A theatrical genre, the drag act, was one of the resources she identified for such subversion: a challenge to the whole way in which the categories of identity are organised, an exposure of the underlying performativity of gender.

At the same time, though, Butler highlighted a potential complication for this view of drag as socially subversive. 'The sight of a transvestite onstage,' she says, 'can compel pleasure and applause while the sight of the same transvestite on the seat next to us on the bus can compel fear, rage, even violence' (Butler 1990: 278). This is no doubt true: theatrical cross-dressing has a long heritage, from the ancient

Greeks to the pantomime dame, and has in the modern era cohabited placidly enough with the very ontology of gender Butler seeks to undo. So there must be something about the onstage situation that negates the disturbing challenge cross-dressing could otherwise produce for our dominant thinking of gender, and to which the violence visited upon offstage transvestites would appear to testify. Butler puts it like this:

> In the theatre, one can say, 'this is just an act,' and de-realize the act, make acting into something quite distinct from what is real. Because of this distinction, one can maintain one's sense of reality in the face of this temporary challenge to our existing ontological assumptions about gender arrangements; the various conventions which announce that 'this is only a play' allows [sic] strict lines to be drawn between the performance and life.
>
> (Butler 1990: 278)

In other words, the critique of gender ontology is in this situation countered by an ontological understanding of theatre, a conception of performance or acting as distinct from and lesser than 'reality' or 'real life'. Nothing that happens onstage is ever more than an illusion, so nothing that happens there need have any consequences for real life. The same ontology allows us to see that the actor or performer exists prior to or underneath the role she or he plays; the role is an act that can be put on and put off at will without ever calling the underlying identity of the performer into question. So while the cross-dressed performer is, on this view, clearly not expressing 'his' or 'her' gender in the performance, the acting of a gender identity on the stage can easily be accounted unreal compared with the 'actual' identity of the person acting it. Offstage, though, these different ontological certainties cannot simply support each other like this. If the person next to us on the bus is not easily classified as just playing a role, then his or her transvestitism becomes more obviously challenging. Since we expect bodily styles off the stage to say something about the identity of the body sporting them, the transvestite in this context lands us in a quandary. Who is this person? From which of their attributes or aspects do we 'read off' their identity? Can identity be read off in such a fashion? How do we understand any such identity to be constituted?

An important implication of Butler's argument here is that if this ontology of gender goes, the parallel ontology of theatrical performance goes with it. If our identities offstage are the product of the various acts through which we become who and what we are, then the notion of an essential person underlying those acts turns out to be merely a socially dominant dissimulation of that process of performative constitution. In which case, the ontological criterion for distinguishing between onstage and offstage, the invocation of this kind of fundamental difference between role-playing and just being ourselves, cannot be upheld. In this context, then, the affinities between Butler's critique of identity and Derrida's deconstructive reading of Austin can be seen once again. As we saw in chapter four, Derrida sought to undermine what had been assumed to be an ontological rendering of the distinction between serious and non-serious performatives; Butler later appropriated this deconstructive intervention for her own purposes. An important consequence of this, though, is that the discussion of non-serious or fictional speech acts by Derrida, Butler, or any number of those who have followed in their footsteps, always starts by presuming that the distinction is primarily drawn by Austin at an ontological level. But the most interesting element in Austin's brief remarks on this point, as I have already had occasion to emphasise, is that it *doesn't* assume that such a difference is necessarily identical with an ontological distinction between 'life' and 'fiction', or between 'reality' and 'illusion'. The hollowness of the non-serious utterance, that is to say, is not easily reduced to the hollowness of mere appearance. If there is such a distinction, and Austin is obviously not denying that there is, then it is to be accounted for in other terms. This kind of ontological criterion will not do the job.

AN ONTOLOGY OF PERFORMANCE?

There is much else in the received wisdom about Austin's comments that needs to be approached warily. One could not seriously argue, for example, that the marking off of some utterances as 'non-serious' constitutes a fully-fledged account even of fiction, let alone of literature, even if Searle seeks to proceed on just such a basis. Neither should we assume that the invocation of seriousness is itself unproblematic, as if its significance and relevance were simply obvious for Austin. It is worth noting that when the word first intrudes into his discussion it is as much cited as used: Austin imagines a potential objection to his account of promising that would demand some more telling indication of seriousness than he is apparently able to guarantee. The quotation marks which accompany its first appearance are scare quotes, too, indicating that Austin himself takes this as a word that ought to be handled with care. Perhaps, then, his use of the term is itself not fully serious. And this first appearance of seriousness can further be read as an explicit questioning of definitions of theatre as mere illusion, his later talk of 'parasites' or 'etiolations' notwithstanding. In the first of his Harvard lectures, he makes clear his rejection of any metaphysical account of utterance that would posit an ontological difference between the inner or essential being of the person speaking and the outwardness of their words. Against this view he asserts that making a 'serious' promise is indeed a matter of saying the right words in the right circumstances, and not 'an inward and spiritual act' that is then outwardly represented or described in the words uttered (Austin 1975: 9). One way his opponents might bolster their position, he suggests, could be to appeal to an ontological conception of theatrical performance for support: the words we speak outwardly would then be like insubstantial words uttered on a stage, merely the image or representation of solid acts *really* done by the 'heart[,] or mind, or other backstage artiste' (Austin 1975: 9–10). In rejecting this position in its entirety, he distances himself from the characterisation of theatrical performance to which it might appeal; indeed, the strangeness of the formulation 'backstage artiste' enhances the sense that this kind of thinking cannot make good its claims. Instead, his argument here insists that our everyday, 'outward' or 'onstage' performances are not to be equated with the insubstantial: we should not imagine or expect to find that our real lives go on somewhere behind or beyond the public stage on which we speak. This is almost a *defence* of theatre against such metaphysical strictures.

That Austin's perspective on theatrical performance cannot be boiled down to a bald distinction between reality and fiction is further demonstrated by his wariness around such a distinction in 'Pretending', the essay in which he made an imprecise beginning on 'the long-term project of classifying and clarifying all possible ways and varieties of *not exactly doing things*' (Austin 1979: 267). Here acting and rehearsing jostle for space among posing, feigning, dissembling, impersonating, imitating, mimicking, shamming, simulating and many kinds of pretending to which they cannot simply be assimilated. Sometimes, for example, pretending to do something can involve 'actually' or 'really' doing it (Austin 1979: 261–62). An undercover police officer on a stake-out may pass his time in pretending to read the newspaper, or in pretending to sweep the road; part of that pretence may well be actually reading the paper or really sweeping the road. Similarly, actors in performance are not always not doing the things they are merely playing at: they cry real tears, for example; sometimes, as in the Michael Winterbottom film, *Nine Songs*, they even have what the papers call 'real sex'. Is such behaviour therefore no different from its accomplishment beyond the frame of performance? The artist Franko B bleeds as part of his performance; Ron Athey cuts or pierces himself and is cut or pierced by his co-performers; Annie Sprinkle famously, notoriously, masturbated to orgasm during her show 'Post Porn Modernist' (see Sprinkle 1998). Clearly there is some kind of difference to be marked here between onstage and offstage behaviour, but equally clearly 'realness' cannot easily be the criterion we want to invoke to mark that difference. For all these reasons, there must be more to the distinction between 'seriousness' and what lies beyond it than a simple boundary between reality and illusion.

To some extent, recent performance theory has been a response to the reworking of the conventions of theatrical or dramatic performance mounted by artists such as these. An important body of feminist theoretical work has reflected profitably not only on what we would ordinarily understand as theatre but also on the performances of figures such as Sprinkle, Karen Finley, Orlan, Angelika Festa and, before them, Carolee Schneemann (see, for example, Phelan 1993, Schneider 1997, Harris 1999). This reflection has found itself working through an understanding of the power and scope of performance, its capacity to challenge the solid world beyond its borders, and its concomitant potential to bring the apparent obviousness of the ways in which those borders are characterised into question. For the American performance theorist Peggy Phelan, at least, this has involved an explicit attempt to formulate a revised 'ontology of performance', an account of how performance in these contexts might properly be understood, in order to clarify such powers (see Phelan 1993: 146–66). For Phelan and others, Butler's work has provided an important resource; but they have also been able to draw on a much more broadly based interrogation of these questions.

For many decades, in fact, a range of practitioners and theorists of drama have drawn on the perhaps unanticipated complexity of 'not exactly doing things', or the inadequacy of any simple opposition between *really* doing or being and *not really* doing or being. The

Western theatre of the late nineteenth century witnessed the rise of a style of theatre that was described as 'naturalist', in which the aim was to break free of the then-dominant conventions of dramatic writing and presentation. One of the means by which this aim was to be realised was through the creation onstage of a convincing representation of the off-stage world. The audience looked at the stage like spectators looking into the frame of a naturalistic, perspectival painting. The actors were doing their best to create lifelike representations of people, inhabiting spaces configured to resemble those inhabited in real life. What one saw onstage, therefore, could be described as an 'iconic sign', a representation that resembled what it stood for. Yet naturalism bred its own discontents: during the earlier decades of the twentieth century, avant-garde practitioners sought to displace this thinking and practice of drama. The German Marxist playwright Bertolt Brecht, for instance, formulated a style of 'epic theatre' that sought precisely to deny the audience the comfortable prospect of entertaining an illusion, of merely watching an apparently lifelike spectacle (Brecht 1964). His audiences were to be encouraged to reflect critically upon what they saw. The drama of the Irish writer Samuel Beckett took its leave of the trappings of earlier styles of performance, and offered fragmented and puzzling plays which would confound demands for the naturalistic representation of character, setting or events. The visionary French writer Antonin Artaud called for the creation of a 'Theatre of Cruelty', in which violence would be done to such demands, and theatre instead would assume a sacred status in developing a connection to the basic well-springs of human life. The whole notion of representation was to be abolished; life was to speak directly through performance. As he said, articulating what he thought of as the distressing condition of contemporary Western humanity, 'I am a man who has lost his life and who is seeking by every means to restore it to its place' (Artaud 1988: 110). An anti-representational theatre was to be one of the most important of those means, and Artaud saw glimpses of it in all sorts of places. The Balinese ritual dancing he witnessed on its performance in Paris in 1931, for example, demonstrated to him that a highly conventional, stylised mode of performance, far from being sterile artifice, could produce something directly striking and meaningful precisely because it was not either given over to narrative or ideas or consumed in producing images of a world that was forever elsewhere (Artaud 1970: 36–49).

HAPPENINGS: PERFORMANCE AS THE THING ITSELF

Artaud's rejection of performance as the illusion or imitation of life, there-fore, was coupled with an insistence on the 'liveness' or 'realness' of perfor-mance itself. Elsewhere, others also began to explore such possibilities. In the America of the 1950s, artists such as Allan Kaprow saw in the 'action painting' of the abstract expressionist Jackson Pollock the prospect of an art that is more practice than object, and the possibility of a kind of per-formance that exceeded the conventional limitations of representational theatre (Kaprow 1993: 1–9). Kaprow began to stage what became known as 'happenings', events or performances in which the staples of theatre, such as narrative, character, setting, and a boundary between playing space and audience, were all abandoned. Performers moved in and through a series of indoor or outdoor spaces, empty lofts or warehouses or courtyards between buildings, rather than on a 'proper' stage; eventually just the street would do. Words might be spoken, costumes worn or actions undertaken, but nothing in a happening was being represented or imitated: there was no illusion for an audience to enter into, and some-times no audience as such at all. Michael Kirby, another practitioner and theorist of happenings, contrasted such performing with the representa-tion of character within the framework, the imagined time and space, of a particular fiction or story. The portrayal of character in this way he called 'matrixed' performance, since it presumed this kind of temporal or spatial 'matrix'. The performer in a happening, on the other hand, did not engage in these ways of fictionalising his or her performance. Instead, it was the 'non-matrixed' performance of actions themselves:

> Let us compare a performer sweeping in a Happening and a performer sweeping in a traditional theatre. The performer in the Happening merely carries out a task. The actor in the traditional play or musical might add character detail: lethargy, vigor, precision, carelessness. He might act 'place': a freezing garret, the deck of a rolling ship, a windy patio. He might convey aspects of the imaginary time situation: how long the character has been sweeping, whether it is early or late.
>
> (Kirby 1965: 17)

Kirby, then, like Artaud, is interested in the possibilities that arise for performance when it is freed of the requirement to represent anything, when the actions of the performer are allowed just to 'be themselves'.

Kaprow's experiments with happenings took these possibilities out beyond the practices envisaged by Kirby. The happening, he concurred, was a mode of performance that could not be set over and against 'reality' as its portrayal or representation: what it offered was 'the certainty of a number of occurrences to which we are more than normally attentive' (Kaprow 1993: 16). A block of ice left to melt slowly in the road could be as much of an 'occurrence' as someone sweeping in a room. As he practised and expounded this mode of performance, then, it became ever more estranged from theatre and increasingly an attitude that might be taken up at any point in ordinary life:

> It is directly involved in the everyday world, ignores theatres and audiences, is more active than meditative, and is close in spirit to physical sports, ceremonies, fairs, mountain climbing, war games, and political demonstrations. It also partakes of the unconscious daily rituals of the supermarket, subway ride at rush hour, and toothbrushing every morning.
>
> (Kaprow 1993: 87)

Art was thus being dissolved back 'into its life sources' (Kaprow 1993: 221), producing a blurring of the distinction between life and the art or performance that could usually be understood as different from it. Kaprow cites Raivo Puusemp as an exemplary practitioner of this blurring, an artist who apparently ran for mayor of the small town of Rosendale, New York in 1975, was elected, and served for two years. This was surely 'real life', yet for Puusemp, Kaprow says, it was also a project, an artwork, a performance: he resigned when he felt the project was complete, rather than finish his term of office. There was no 'audience' for this, either: what he had done was only publicised afterwards, and then reluctantly (Kaprow 1993: 209–11). What made it an artwork was just the attitude adopted towards the election campaign and the subsequent period in office, or the decision to designate it as a performance.

For others who continued to work within and around the recognisable conventions of theatrical performance, the transformation of drama in the happenings and elsewhere left an indelible mark. The director and theorist Richard Schechner, who worked in the New York of the 1960s and 1970s with a company called 'The Performance Group', set out his understanding of the relations between such key terms as drama, script, theatre and performance. He imagined a model of four concentric discs or circles, stacked so that the biggest provides a base and each of the others rests on the one immediately larger than itself. The smallest circle he called the drama, by which he meant the components of the event as a whole that could be captured in a written text and carried or transmitted from one place and time to another. The next largest he called, slightly misleadingly, the script: this was 'the basic code of the events', again transmissible from place to place, but now including patterns of action that are not written down but transmitted from person to person. Surrounding this was theatre, 'the event enacted by a specific group of performers', the particular form of a production. At the bottom, encompassing all this, was what he called performance: 'the whole constellation of events, most of them passing unnoticed, that take place in/among both performers and audience from the time the first spectator enters the field of the performance – the precinct where the theatre takes place – to the time the last spectator leaves' (Schechner 1988: 72). This would include, then, not just what happened between the raising and lowering of a curtain or between two blackouts, but also all the preparatory interactions between spectators and the performance space, and anything that happened in and around that space until the last audience member departed. In some of his productions Schechner sought to explore this region by leaving performers *in situ* to interact with audience members during an interval, for example, and by allowing contact between audience and cast prior to the acting out of the play. For Schechner, performance was emphatically not just what happened in a clearly demarcated stage space: in using the term to denote also the whole range of experiences that surround the site and duration of theatre he was opening up 'matrixed' performance to the 'non-matrixed' interactions that surround it.

So in these contexts there is a notable lack of what might be imagined to be a secure distinction between theatre and life, between performance onstage and a reality subsisting beyond it. This kind of insight has also provided impetus for performance artists keen to explore the capacities and limits of the performing body without confining that performance to established or recognised practices like acting or dance, or to conventional sites. The body displayed in performance art need not be understood as engaged in a specialised form of representation, one beyond the significances that our bodies can bear in ordinary or everyday life. If anything, it goes the other way: it has sometimes been argued that the naked body in performance, in particular, or the body marked or pierced, can enact a corporeal, psychic reality that is often concealed in the everyday. It can thus show the everyday what is usually hidden, but is nonetheless always there. Not everyone has been convinced by the claims to immediacy that sometimes characterise this kind of thinking about performance: the critic Philip Auslander, for example, has questioned the theoretical viability of attempts to define performance as a kind of 'being live' that can securely oppose itself to modes or technologies of representation, whether they be old-fashioned writing or the newer digital media (Auslander 1999); Derrida, too, explored what seemed to him to be the contradictions in Artaud's pursuit of a theatre that might be redeemed from the inauthenticity of representation (Derrida 1978: 169–95, 232–50). Such criticisms, though, do not therefore seek to re-establish some kind of ontological divide between the emptiness of performance, on the one hand, and the substantiality of the real, on the other: rather, they suggest that such substance is not what characterises the experience we call real life, much as Derrida claimed that citationality was as much a feature of 'serious' speech acts as it was of their 'non-serious' counterparts.

PERFORMING LIFE

These theoretical and practical developments in theatre found intellectual support in some influential tendencies in sociology and anthropology. Both of these disciplines might be expected to take an interest in theatre, specifically, or in performance more generally, since performing is both a distinctive part of modern Western society and an element in non-Western cultures that the West has often regarded with fascination, as Artaud's interest in Balinese dance shows. The work of the American sociologist Erving Goffman, particularly his 1959 book *The Presentation of Self in Everyday Life*, presented an account of social action that was predicated on a notion of performance. In their ordinary lives, Goffman argued, people played out roles: they were not consciously 'acting' or 'pretending', necessarily, nor did they simply choose which role they would play and how; but in order to take up any social position, something like role-playing was required. That is to say, in order to be a policeman, perhaps, or a bus conductor, it is necessary to put on a recognisable, distinctive costume or uniform, to carry oneself in a certain way, even to speak in an appropriate tone and use the 'right' vocabulary. And this is something that people do all the time, in our public or professional lives, certainly, but also in what we might think of as more private or informal contexts. For example, attending a funeral, a visit to the opera, or a meal at a restaurant all depend on certain established ways of behaving, although some are more tightly conventional than others. Woe betide the mourner who greets the bereaved with a cheery smile, or the diner at a Michelin-starred restaurant who burps loudly after her or his main course. These roles form the basis for the ways in which we navigate round our social world, improvising scenes from the array of narrative possibilities and forms that are available to us. As Goffman famously put it:

> Ordinary social intercourse is itself put together as a scene is put together, by the exchange of dramatically inflated actions, counteractions, and terminating replies. Scripts even in the hands of unpractised players can come to life because life itself is a dramatically enacted thing. All the world is not, of course, a stage, but the crucial ways in which it isn't are not easy to specify.
>
> (Goffman 1959: 72)

In this last sentence, we can detect a certain hesitancy in Goffman's account of the relation between theatre and everyday life. Is the language of theatricality that Goffman uses being offered as an analogical framework, as if something about ordinary life could be revealed by stressing its resemblance to theatre in important aspects? Or is this a more substantial claim, prefiguring Butler to some degree, about the fundamental performativity, in a dramatic sense, of our lives? And if so, then how can the relation of everyday to theatrical performance, and more importantly the difference between them, be understood?

For the anthropologist Victor Turner, human life was necessarily performative, in the sense of being a set of active processes. Where other anthropologists of the post-war period sought to analyse culture as an abstract, sometimes static structure of signs, he understood it instead as an ongoing work or action. In particular, his theoretical analyses focused on what he called 'social drama'. By this he meant the dynamic process through which a particular social unit, a family, community or institution, would experience a breach of its integrity or order and consequently fall into crisis as increasing polarisation and factionalism made the initial disharmony more severe. An attempt would then be made to grasp the situation through redressive procedures designed to heal the breach. The social unit might manage to reintegrate itself once again through these procedures; if it did not, it would be forced to acknowledge the division as irreparable (Turner 1974: 37–41). So in this way, too, Turner took the crises of everyday life to exhibit something of the characteristics of theatre in acting out what looked like recognisable plot structures. These kinds of plots were not fictions: their unfolding just is the way in which a social unit deals with the antagonisms and difficulties that beset it. As in Goffman's account, this kind of role-playing makes a difference to people's lives. The ways in which meaning is made over time in drama are therefore akin to the processes through which societies create and recreate themselves.

In more recent years, other theorists have asserted the performative nature of the everyday from different perspectives. Jon McKenzie, for example, has outlined a view of performance as an existential category through which human identities and activities are coming to be shaped (McKenzie 2001). Performance for McKenzie encompasses the sense of social drama that Turner outlined and that performance studies has taken up, but he seeks also to link this way of thinking to other modes of life in which performance has become an organising mode. In particular, he draws attention to the ways in which our lives are lived through an understanding of performance as the *efficiency* of a particular institutional system or one of its elements, like a business or an economy. There is also, crucially, the notion of technological performance, the *effectiveness* of machines or instruments at performing particular functions (McKenzie 2001: 27–136). If everyday life is performative, then, it is performative in all these ways. A teacher, for example, may be engaging in performance in a quasi-dramatic sense when she inhabits that particular role and performs her social function according to its requirements; yet if her salary is to some extent dependent on the measured exam results achieved by the school – if, in other words, she receives 'performance-related pay' – then her actions are also ordered according to this other paradigm of performance. Her life as a teacher is structured so as to ensure that outputs, in this case exam results, are maximised. In a similar way, the lives of factory and office workers have been shaped by the need for efficient performance since assembly lines were first reorganised to take account of the earliest time-and-motion studies. And insofar as our lives have evolved, and continue to evolve, in formative proximity to all manner of technological apparatuses, this sense of effective performance plays a crucial part in making us who we are. In McKenzie's view, then, speaking of the processes or actions of everyday life as a kind of performance means invoking much more than the dramatic paradigm.

For Dwight Conquergood, though, the attention that the study of performance has necessarily brought to bear on the bodily, practical and processual nature of human existence presents an ongoing challenge to any attempts to marginalise it as the knowledge of a special province of human activity. He sees in such attention the raising to academic visibility of a whole way of living and knowing human lives that has been repressed by the standard Western accounts of what knowledge is: performance is actually a way of living that we have somehow repressed or forgotten. As he puts it:

> The dominant way of knowing in the academy is that of empirical observation and critical analysis from a distanced perspective: 'knowing that,' and 'knowing about.' This is a view from above the object of inquiry: knowledge that is anchored in paradigm and secured in print. This propositional knowledge is shadowed by another way of knowing that is grounded in active, intimate, hands-on participation and personal connection: 'knowing how,' and 'knowing who.' This is a view from ground level, in the thick of things. This is knowledge that is anchored in practice and circulated within a performance community, but is ephemeral.
>
> (Conquergood 2002: 146)

The dominant sense of how and what we might know, therefore, neglects or erases a 'whole realm of complex, finely nuanced meaning that is embodied, tacit, intoned, gestured, improvised, coexperienced, covert' (Conquergood 2002: 146). This realm, invisible to a Western way of knowing that has refused to see or acknowledge it, is the practical knowledge through which corporeal lives are lived. Its opposition to the dominant mode has been worked out particularly starkly in the forms of resistance that non-Western peoples offered to the colonial project of mapping, classifying and controlling their societies. Because performance studies attends to our lives as practice, as embodied, in the way that it does, it is well placed to insist on the importance of these other, marginalised, 'nonserious' (Conquergood 2002: 146) modes of experience, modes whose marginality is a function not of their insignificance but of their repression.

PERFORMANCE, RITUAL AND PLAY

In these different accounts of everyday life as a kind of performance we can see a shared insistence that the kind of performance usually associated with theatre *matters*. It has effects, it shapes societies, it is the very stuff of our ordinary lives. This is very far, now, from any sense of performing as illusion, the pale imitation of a real life lived elsewhere. If performance matters, it is because it is in a crucial sense infrastructural: it is fundamental to the constitution of our social and cultural world. As Turner suggests, 'if man is a sapient animal, a toolmaking animal, a self-making animal, a symbol-using animal, he is, no less, a performing animal, *Homo performans*' (Turner 1987: 81). The resort to the concept of performance is therefore an attempt to put in place an understanding of what we really are. To this extent, it offers an alternative social ontology, one that does not reduce performance to a merely secondary status; and because it asserts that we become what we are only through our actions it also challenges the very categories of ontology, as Butler's critique of the notion of fixed identities and essential natures shows. There is here, too, a renewed resemblance to Austin. In particular, Conquergood's championing of performance as a mode or genre of knowledge that is neglected or denigrated by dominant Western conceptions of 'propositional knowledge' recalls Austin's own championing of a thinking anchored in the pragmatic dimension, in language in *action*, against the inability of a philosophy in the grip of the 'descriptive fallacy' even to acknowledge its claims.

The insistence on the importance of performance, then, goes hand in hand with a determination to challenge the terms through which it has been denigrated. If performance matters, then, it matters in a distinctive way. This distinctiveness is an issue elsewhere, too, because an emphasis on the infrastructural nature of performance in everyday life is often also coupled, and not always easily, with a continuing recognition of or insistence on the peculiar functions or scope of performing. Performance theory therefore does not necessarily seek to strip performing of the characteristics that might be read as signs of its separation from the everyday; instead, it offers a new perspective on precisely these characteristics. Consider, for example, the analysis of play and ritual that performance theorists such as Turner and Schechner have developed from the model offered by the early twentieth century Dutch historian Johan Huizinga, whose seminal study of play, *Homo Ludens*, was first published in 1938. In his analysis, Huizinga emphasised what he called the 'formal characteristics' of play, suggesting that it is 'a free activity standing quite consciously outside "ordinary" life as being "not serious", but at the same time absorbing the player intensely and utterly. It is an activity connected with no material interest, and no profit can be gained by it' (Huizinga 1950: 13). So play is understood as a time and place apart from the everyday, a separate space where actions unfold according to a different logic and without reference to the demands or constraints of ordinary life. Huizinga, though, goes on to relate play to ritual, which he sees as a kind of activity apart from the everyday that does not thereby become 'not serious'. Victor Turner draws on Huizinga in presenting a theory of ritual in the light of his theory of social drama. He does not claim that ritual is simply part of the everyday, recognising instead its distinctiveness as a time apart. He does acknowledge, though, that it has a particular social function to discharge. Crucial to this is its capacity to transform some or all of its participants: they are not the same at the conclusion of the ritual as they were at its beginning, as a couple undergoing a wedding are transformed by the process. Ritual is therefore a rite of passage, a process which makes a difference in the society or culture in which it is enacted (Turner 1969).

For Turner, borrowing his terms from the French ethnographer Arnold van Gennep, the fact that ritual involves a transformation or transition in the status of its participants means that it can be understood as a liminal process. Ritual is liminal because it takes its participants across a 'limen', or threshold, from one status or identity to another. Thus, for example, an initiation rite takes a child or children across the threshold between childhood and adulthood. The liminal phase occurs when the participants have been stripped of their old identities and are yet to be confirmed in their new ones, when they are 'betwixt and between', as Turner put it (Turner 1969: 95). The liminal phase is a moment of fluidity, and Turner therefore associates it with the possibility of creativity, of invention or innovation. The liminal moment is the moment of 'anti-structure', 'when the past is momentarily negated, suspended or abrogated, and the future has not yet begun, an instant of pure potentiality when everything, as it were, trembles in the balance' (Turner 1982: 44). So the relationship between ritual process and the everyday is a complicated one: it stands apart, like the non-serious interludes of play, but it also has the function of enacting changes in status which relate directly to the everyday world. At the same time, it not only discharges this function but also hints at possible changes and transformations of the society in which it works, and here it manifests some of the radical freedom from responsibility associated with play. Ritual performance is therefore itself something of a liminal entity: it is 'both earnest and playful' (Turner 1982: 35), preserving the apartness and openness of the non-serious while also managing to make a difference in the world of the everyday.

This openness or playfulness leads Turner to describe the liminality of ritual in grammatical terms, as action in the 'subjunctive mood'. The 'indicative mood' describes verbs in clauses that refer to an actual state of affairs, as in the sentence 'I am angry'. Verbs in the subjunctive mood are used when the clause or sentence is casting doubt on, or supposing, or imagining, the state of affairs of which it speaks, as in 'I would be angry if I were you'. As Turner suggests, 'the subjunctive . . . is always concerned with "wish, desire, possibility or hypothesis"; it is a world of "as if", ranging from scientific hypothesis to festive fantasy. It is "as if it *were* so," not "it *is* so"' (Turner 1982: 83). The invocation of the possible, this invitation to fantasise or imagine, might be seen as marking the distance of the subjunctive liminal from the indicative everyday. Yet the social efficacy of ritual, its power to accomplish permanent changes, ensures that this moment of the 'as if' is not to be written off as simply 'not real'.

LIMINALITY AND THEATRE

Neither Turner nor Schechner considered what happens in modern Western theatre to be liminal in precisely this sense. Instead, Turner coined the term 'liminoid' to describe these kinds of performance. They are understood as having a family resemblance to ritual processes, but are not such processes themselves: they do not have the same claim as rituals on societies or cultures as a whole; they are much more clearly commodities that can be taken or left as individual preference dictates (Turner 1982: 20–59). To this extent, they belong to that part of our lives that the modern West has marked off as leisure rather than work; they are what an audience might watch for entertainment. But this disengagement from social centrality has not necessarily been understood as a kind of powerlessness. Schechner has traced out what he calls the 'efficacy-entertainment braid' through the range of liminal and liminoid performances, where 'efficacy' denotes the power of the performance to make a difference, and 'entertainment' by contrast indicates performances whose primary purpose is to be enjoyed as some kind of spectacle (Schechner 1988: 106–52). Ritual and theatre, or liminal and liminoid performances, all combine these two aspects to some degree; there is, Schechner says, no performance that is purely efficacious or pure entertainment. In the avant-garde theatre in which he worked, for instance, an emphasis was placed on the 'transformative' potential of the performance, its capacity to work changes upon performers and audiences, even though it had no 'proper' ritual function (Schechner 1988: 121). Rituals, too, allow space for the pleasures of display or of witnessing the acts performed.

It is also possible, according to Schechner, for something of the subjunctive character of liminality to carry across into liminoid performance. The behaviour undertaken in all our performances, he says, is 'restored behaviour', which is as much as to say with Goffman, Butler and others that it is conventional or citational, following established patterns, habits or customs (Schechner 1985). In theatre and other kinds of peculiar performance, 'strips' of such behaviour, like strips of film, are cut out of ordinary life, recombined and rehearsed to present new assemblages or combinations. This means that all behaviour has something of the 'as if', something of the subjunctive about it; in performance, and particularly in the rehearsal process that acutely mobilises the possibilities of restored behaviour, there is an 'in-between' quality to the actions in which performers engage. Schechner describes such liminality as *transitional*, suspended between 'my' behaviour and that which I am citing or imitating:

> During workshops-rehearsals performers play with words, things, and actions, some of which are 'me' and some 'not me'. By the end of the process the 'dance goes into the body.' So Olivier is not Hamlet, but he is also not not Hamlet. The reverse is also true: in this production of the play, Hamlet is not Olivier, but he is also not not Olivier. Within this field or frame of double negativity choice and virtuality remain activated.
>
> (Schechner 1985: 110)

In this situation, then, there is a kind of grey area, a border zone, where performance takes place. The performer behaves 'as if' she or he were someone else, but in doing so also lays claim to that someone else, performing the 'not me' and the 'not not me' simultaneously. This behaviour is neither actually mine, nor merely a fiction. The actor Laurence Olivier, to use Schechner's example, can still be differentiated from the Hamlet he plays; but this differentiation has to be qualified by the peculiar recognition that in playing 'his' Hamlet, he is also *not just* not Hamlet. If we were looking to combine these aspects in one claim, we could perhaps say that when he plays the part, Olivier is *not exactly* being Hamlet, and *not exactly* being himself.

The subjunctive, liminal nature of theatre emerges here not so much in a secure difference from the settled, certain and actual, but more in its capacity to corrode any such assertion of a secure difference. As Schechner says,

> Olivier will not be interrupted in the middle of 'To be or not to be' and asked, 'Whose words are those?' And if he were interrupted, what could his reply be? The words belong, or don't belong, equally to Shakespeare, Hamlet, Olivier.
>
> (Schechner 1985: 111)

At the same time, though, we might feel that such a question cannot simply be refused in this way or declared unintelligible. If the 'as if' is not safely or easily marked off, 'de-realized', as Butler put it, but persists as the place and point where such boundaries become hard to pin down, then one consequence will be precisely that we will not easily know on every occasion whether or not a question such as 'whose words are those?' can be legitimately posed or comfortably answered.

Schechner himself, as Butler notes, has given this issue some thought in describing the activities of Squat, a theatre group in New York who presented their performances in a space that had previously been used as a shop (Schechner 1985: 298–311; Butler 1990: 278). The space was arranged such that the performance took place just inside the shop, with the audience further inside; behind the performers, therefore, and in full view of the audience, was the plate glass window onto the street beyond. Performances were regularly punctuated by events taking place outside, which may or may not have been part of the show; similarly, an audience often gathered beyond the window, looking in, and were therefore themselves on display for the audience 'proper' inside. When an ambulance pulled up outside, or police entered the building and walked into the performance space, were the people in these 'roles' part of the performance? When they spoke, as they did, did those words count within or beyond the onstage world? Was it immediately obvious whether that was an appropriate question or not?

Schechner himself speaks of these performances as experimenting with the boundary between 'life' and 'art' (Schechner 1985: 304–5). He has also characterised analogous kinds of performing as 'dark play', 'playing in the dark when some or all of the players don't know that they are playing' (Schechner 1993: 36). Such terms query the notion that some kind of simply given frame surrounds play, or pretence, or the 'as if', with steady borders. Performance theory in this mode is marked by two not always complementary impulses: on the one hand, the insistence that any boundary between the performances of 'life' and 'art' is shifting and arbitrary (Schechner 1988: 71, 85), but on the other, the detailed analysis of the range and variety of ways the difference can be both posited and enacted. The distinction between seriousness and the non-serious cannot be dispensed with, without losing all sense of how the suspensions of the indicative mood that give performance its peculiarity might be understood. At the same time, play cannot be separated out as pure weightlessness, the frictionless or inconsequential recombination or rehearsal of elements in our everyday lives without denying the ways in which its subjunctive power challenges such a separation. The anthropological focus on ritual matters, then, precisely because it appears to provide an instance within which these different capabilities or understandings can be reconciled. Yet even here the dichotomy will not simply be transcended. We can see this in the way that Schechner is drawn to braid

together the categories of 'efficacy' and 'entertainment': having alighted
on ritual as a resolving instance, he then brings back the disjunction by
arguing that every ritual practice is braided in this fashion.

LIFE, ART AND THE NON-SERIOUS

This interest in the transformative power of ritual demonstrates the
affinity between the performance theorists' account of performative processes and the way of thinking about performativity that has been pursued in my previous chapters. Austin's own formulation of the speech
act included the kinds of things done in ritual or ceremonial among his
clearest examples, and his vocabulary has offered a basis for subsequent
anthropological analyses of such processes (see Tambiah 1985). Yet the
performance theorists' approach to the difficulties of separating out seriousness and the non-serious, life and art, might well be seen to reflect
back on the way that Austin invokes that distinction. As we have seen,
he shares their sense that we are not talking here about a differentiation
between reality and illusion, and that this kind of ontological claim will
not do. But a simple appeal to conventions or to criteria will not substitute for it either. The reason that the non-serious performative is *'in a
peculiar way* hollow or void' (Austin 1975: 22) is not that it violates any
particular felicity condition or criterion of validity. It is more that the
conditions as a whole are somehow articulated so that the usual consequences, such as a change in status for the speaker, his or her openness
to new responsibilities and new demands for accountability, do not simply follow. The performance theorists' sense that this articulation of conditions is itself a fraught business, that the 'as if' exceeds its proper
limits, that what we call 'performance' marks precisely the persistence
of this excess, returns to Austin his sense of peculiarity. When Hamlet
promises to remember and avenge his father, he begins to feel the tight-
ening bonds of a commitment he will then have difficulty discharging;
when Olivier promises to buy someone a drink, he too is answerable for
his words. If Olivier is not exactly being Hamlet, though, the clarity of
these situations is not easily apparent. And since this 'not exactly'
emphasises the lack of any securely ontological either/or, no simple
invocation of reality will settle matters for us.

What is shown up acutely here is precisely the *challenge* of seriousness. From Austin's perspective, if confusion can arise it is because a

promise, for example, invokes the conditions and implications of a promise wherever it is uttered. But if the possibility of non-seriousness is always with us even when it is apparently ruled out, so is the possibility of seriousness. I could always be joking or quoting, for example, when I tell airport security that I have a bomb in my luggage, even though it is expressly asserted that such assertions will be taken seriously. (But can they *really* mean it? Regular incidents at airports round the world suggest that even if they *cannot*, somehow they do.) As I am carted off, perhaps I could try appealing to the iterability of the mark in mitigation (see Culler 1983: 124–25); it would do me no good. This, though, would not be because the enforcers of this law have not read enough Derrida. On the contrary: if there is a law here to which my custodians will appeal, it is a law that exists in all its absurdity precisely because no infallible grounds for determining the difference between the serious and the non-serious can otherwise be invoked. The issue is clearly as pressing, if less stark, elsewhere. When I promised to lend you some money, was I joking, or not exactly promising? What about the utterance would be different if I was? But if non-seriousness needs to be acknowledged in this way, then even such commitments as promising cannot depend just on a conformity to conventions: they will continue to be excessive, demanding a response from us that is not just procedural. Being serious, that is to say, is also a matter of acknowledging a responsibility for our words, a responsibility that exceeds rules because rules are fragile in just this fashion. Contrary to the way he is usually read, Austin was not proposing a simplistic *answer* to this problem, a way of sorting out seriousness once and for all so that such responsibility could be deflected onto a theory of speech acts instead. His distinction between serious and non-serious utterances, together with his sense that there was something peculiar about this distinction, are instead the beginnings of an acknowledgment of the question, and acknowledging too the consequences it has for how we might think about what it is to perform, to do things with words, the way we do.

'OPEN THE CAGE AND LET US OUT'

An example can illustrate the ways in which the theory and practice of contemporary performance resonates with this particular complex of issues. In 1992–93, the Latino performance artists Guillermo

Gómez-Peña and Coco Fusco presented a piece entitled *Two Undiscovered Amerindians Visit ...* in Madrid, London, Sydney, Minneapolis, Washington, Chicago and New York. The choice of locations was not arbitrary: 1992 was the five hundredth anniversary of Columbus's first voyage to the 'New World', and the cities chosen were all in countries heavily if variously implicated in European colonialism. Taking exception to the celebratory recycling of Eurocentric myths that the anniversary called forth, Fusco and Gómez-Peña decided to present themselves as a pair of 'Guatinauis', the only lately 'discovered' Amerindian inhabitants of a fictional island in the Gulf of Mexico. To this end, they dressed themselves in parodic 'native costumes', and carried on their daily routine within the confines of a 12-foot square cage for the amusement or enlightenment of Western spectators. There were sober information boards alongside the cage, one a mocked up encyclopaedia entry showing the location of their island. They had 'zoo guards' to watch over them and interact with the public, while also feeding them sandwiches and fruit and escorting them on leashes when they needed to leave the cage. For a donation, Fusco would dance to a hip-hop accompaniment, while Gómez-Peña would recite apparently traditional stories in a nonsense language, and both would pose for photos; in New York, a glimpse of 'authentic Guatinaui male genitals' could be secured for $5 (Fusco 1994: 145). This was not the only detail of the performance that pushed the parodic nature of the enterprise to the fore: from the activities carried on in the cage, the spectator would come to imagine that the traditional tasks of these 'primitive' Amerindians included sewing voodoo dolls, lifting weights, and using a laptop.

Only in New York did the performance take place in a gallery. Elsewhere, it was presented in public squares or museums of natural history. For the two artists, the point was precisely to draw attention to the long Western history of displaying non-Western peoples as spectacles for entertainment or specimens for classification, a history going back to the earliest years of transatlantic exploration and settlement. Displaying the exotic foreigner in this way, the artists argued, was a key means whereby Europe exerted control over the territories and peoples it managed to conquer. Both the disinterested gaze of the European anthropologist and the merely curious gaze of a European public eager for novelty were in fact heavily implicated in the establishment of these peoples as dominated animals or objects. The dioramas of

the natural history museum and the spectacles of the freak show or travelling circus therefore took their not too dissimilar places in this colonialist history. Presenting their own performance in such institutions, or
in the public squares of European cities, would 'cite' that history as a
step towards bringing it out into the open, an important corrective to
the dominant narrative of the colonial projects inaugurated by
Columbus's voyage. Yet it would also deprive the spectators of the kind
of frame provided by the gallery or the theatre for artworks or performances. The performance would not obviously be marked as theatre or
art. The passing public would be challenged when they looked on, and
when they were brought to interact with the performers or their
'guards'. As Fusco later put it:

> We chose not to announce the event through prior publicity or any
> other means, when it was possible to exert such control; we intended
> to create a surprise or 'uncanny' encounter, one in which audiences
> had to undergo their own process of reflection as to what they were
> seeing, aided only by written information and parodically didactic
> zoo guards. In such encounters with the unexpected, people's
> defense mechanisms are less likely to operate with their normal effi-
> ciency; caught off guard, their beliefs are more likely to rise to the
> surface.
>
> (Fusco 1994: 148)

The hope, in other words, was that the spectators would respond in
ways that the piece would then require them to question: they would
have to take responsibility for, and therefore come to examine, the
underlying attitudes and assumptions with which Fusco and Gómez-
Peña were able to confront them. 'As we assumed the stereotypical role
of the domesticated savage,' Fusco suggested, 'many audience members
felt entitled to assume the role of the colonizer, only to find themselves
uncomfortable with the implications of the game' (Fusco 1994: 152).

From the beginning, though, the responses of those drawn to engage
with the performance varied wildly. Some were only too happy to read
the Guatinauis as animals or objects of fun, to grope them, to feed them
bananas through the bars or make monkey noises at them, without
seeming to want to confront the implications of behaving in this dehu-
manising fashion. The alarming ease with which this happened led

Fusco to the conclusion that 'colonialist roles have been internalized quite effectively', even in a United States that is reluctant to see itself as an imperial entity (Fusco 1994: 153). More arresting than this, though, was the surprisingly large number of people – over fifty per cent, Fusco estimated – who took the performance literally, believing that they really were looking at two undiscovered Amerindians. Of these, most were shockingly unshocked, as if the public display of human beings in a cage was nothing to be worried about. Others took to remonstrating angrily with the guards, insisting that the captives be let out, while a proportion attempted to sympathise with the imprisoned 'primitives'. Even though the performance was neither marked as 'art' nor presented in a standard art context, Fusco and Gómez-Peña expressed surprise at this level of credulity. After all, details such as the laptop and music indicated that this was a parodic rendering of such ethnographic display, and its assimilation to the conventions of animal exhibition was a none-too-subtle pointer towards the kind of critical reflection that they hoped to provoke. The artists found this response somewhat distracting. For one thing, it gave those who might feel uncomfortable around this performance the option of accusing it of dishonestly passing itself off as something it was not: the moral and political accusations levelled by Fusco and Gómez-Peña could be obscured with a different set aimed squarely at them. Fusco therefore suggested that, in the end, 'trying to determine who really believes the fiction and who doesn't became less significant for us in the course of this performance than figuring out what the audience's sense of the rules of the game and their role in it was' (Fusco 1994: 158).

The power of this suggestion is that it directs attention away from the question 'real or not?' towards the rather different issue of the various normative frameworks that this performance could offer its audience to structure their interaction with it. The difficulty, though, is that an understanding of 'the rules of the game' cannot simply take the place of an accompanying understanding of the seriousness of what is being witnessed. The question of whether the performance was an instance of falsehood may indeed be a distraction, but whether or not the Guatinauis counted as undiscovered Amerindians for those who met them is less obviously irrelevant. To describe the interactions made possible by the performance as a game highlights this: whether or not you are only playing at treating me like an animal, whether or not we're sure that we're only playing, might well matter if we are to understand our relation to each other in this situation. The question is therefore not really why or how some people came to take the performance 'seriously': the issue rather is what in fact it *is* to take it seriously, to let it weigh upon us as something that obliges, demanding a certain kind of response. In responding we cannot put ourselves beyond role-playing, since the framework of what we call conventions and roles is precisely integral to the normativity of the lives we lead together. To feel an obligation here, though, is to register both the demands such frameworks make on us and the sense that such frameworks are not necessarily enough to guarantee the validity of those demands. This, needless to say, can be a peculiar business, especially when – as here, and as in prominent currents in modern and contemporary performance – measures are taken to create something uncanny. A number of the zoo guards apparently found the whole experience too disconcerting to be bearable, struggling with what from one direction might seem like a perfectly trivial and blameless complicity. When asked on a later occasion what his 'ideal spectator' would do in the face of their performance, Gómez-Peña suggested that she or he would 'open the cage and let us out' (Taylor 1998: 169). For witnesses to the performance to respond in such a fashion would require of them a delicate balance of different moments or levels of seriousness and play, different kinds of response. There could be no guarantee that such a balance would be achievable or sustainable: given that this ideal spectator would be one who refused to countenance what the work offered, we might well expect it not to be.

In the kind of situation established by this performance, then, and in the terms we might use to register how it does its work, we can find ourselves echoing the cluster of issues that have often arisen in the context of the debates around performativity. This is not a simple correspondence: there are of course other ways of talking about performance, other dimensions to this theoretical project. If the proximity between theories of performance and performativity is to amount to anything very much, the light that each term can shed on the other will have to be a continuing point of reference. Yet that proximity will only be genuinely interesting if we acknowledge the extent to which the theoretical work on performativity has not simply added up to a single, easily assimilable idea. Invoking it brings us not the safety of an answer but the ongoing pressure of a question. To see this, though, we perhaps need to get past my initial claim that the history of the performative can actually be a history of something as simple as a concept. As I hope I have shown, and both Austin and Derrida were more than happy to suggest, it is all a bit more complicated, and a bit more interesting, than that.

GLOSSARY

Constative In Austin's initial classification of utterances, 'constative' was used to describe utterances such as statements, descriptions, and assertions. The constative was thus an utterance that purported to describe the world, rather than an action in its own right. In the course of his Harvard lectures, Austin gives up this formulation in favour of the category of the speech act; stating and describing therefore become varieties of speech act, rather than a kind of speaking that is to be opposed to acting.

Deconstruction The term is most closely associated with the work of the French philosopher Jacques Derrida, though it was also claimed by related thinkers such as the American critic Paul de Man. Deconstruction is notoriously and rightly difficult to sum up or define, since the kind of work gathered under this title resists its reduction to a concept or idea. It is perhaps best described as a work of desedimentation or unsettling, a kind of putting in motion of the very categories or presuppositions underpinning the projects of philosophy or theory.

Descriptive fallacy For Austin, a mistaken vision of language that he attributes to the dominant philosophical trends of his day, particularly logical positivism, in which language is seen primarily as a means of describing the world, and sentences are accordingly seen primarily as statements.

Felicity For Austin, any speech act can be assessed as either 'felicitous' or 'infelicitous'. A felicitous speech act is one that is valid or appropriate: it accords with conventional procedures and the other pragmatic conditions that allow something to be done through the saying of a particular set of words. Thus an order would be felicitous if it used the right words and was said by an appropriate person to someone who was in a position to receive it as such. All speech acts can be assessed, Austin claims, in terms of their felicity: thus even the assessment of the truth or falsity of a statement also involves the pragmatic conditions in which it is issued. In some circumstances, a statement such as 'France is hexagonal' can count as true or felicitous; in others, it cannot.

Happening In the third quarter of the twentieth century, a number of theatre practitioners and artists in Europe and America began to produce events or performances which dispensed with some or all of the normal requirements of drama, such as character, plot, script, even audience. Such performances were termed *Happenings*: they were not representations or imitations of either an imaginary world or a real world beyond the theatre; they were events in their own right.

Illocution, illocutionary force   In Austin and subsequent speech act theory, the illocutionary force of any utterance is the function it performs or the effect it achieves *in* being said, such as promising, threatening, ordering, requesting or declaring. Illocutionary force is achieved when the utterance conforms to established conventional procedures and other felicity conditions for any function of this sort. It is to be distinguished from perlocution.

Interpellation   In the account of ideology developed by the French Marxist philosopher Louis Althusser, 'interpellation' denotes the process whereby a subject takes on its discrete identity in response to being addressed in particular terms by the dominant ideological forces in a society. He likens the process to the experience of hearing a policeman shout 'hey you!' and turning in response: when we turn, we respond as the person hailed, even if the shout was not aimed specifically at us. We are thus singled out, identified, in responding.

Iterability   Derrida argues that all marks or signifying elements – characters, words, sentences, pictures, hieroglyphs, gestures, uniforms and so on – must be repeatable or iterable; they must be able to function beyond a particular context or situation if they are to count as marks at all. A non-iterable mark just would not be a mark; it would not be able to signify or stand for something since it would not be recognisable as an element in a language, a code or a system of signs. But the iterable mark therefore combines sameness and difference in a combination that is not necessarily stable: without being iterable, no mark could ever mean the same thing in different contexts; yet because it is iterable, a mark can never be constrained to signify a single meaning.

Logical positivism   A dominant movement in Anglo-American philosophy in the early decades of the twentieth century, which set out both to clarify the logical structure of natural language and to confine philosophy within its proper limits. According to this way of thinking, philosophy was equipped only to make claims about the logic of language; all claims about the world were claims that could only meaningfully be made if they could also be empirically verified by broadly scientific means. Metaphysical claims about the ultimate structure of reality, aesthetic judgements and moral arguments that could not be verified in this fashion were and therefore among the higher species of nonsense.

Ordinary language philosophy For Austin, and for followers of his approach such as Stanley Cavell, ordinary language is the primary resource for philosophical work. In attending carefully to the kinds of discrimination that were made possible in 'natural' or 'given' languages spoken beyond the specific contexts of philosophy, we might be able to reflect critically on the claims of philosophy itself, and to rearticulate the basis on which philosophy might seek to justify its claims. The problem with much of the analytical work that prevailed in Anglo-American philosophy, for Austin, was that it often set out from what it took to be the ordinary uses of words, but did not often stop to examine this usage closely enough. Thus it erected elaborate accounts of, for example, perception, which depended for their plausibility on a way of using ordinary perception-language that actual attention to 'what we say' in relevant situations would not support. While Austin's brand of ordinary language philosophy was influential, it was not the only body of work to which the term was applied: the later philosophy of Ludwig Wittgenstein, for example, has sometimes been described in similar terms, even though it is in many ways very different indeed.

Performative (1) In Austin's early formulation, an utterance that performs a particular action rather than a description. Saying 'I order you to peel the potatoes' does not describe the action of ordering: it *is* that action. Initially contrasted with 'constative', though the contrast is later replaced by the account of the 'speech act'. (2) The speech act can also be described as a performative or a 'performative utterance', without necessarily implying a contrast with the constative. (3) In performance theory, an adjective that can be applied to the dramatic or theatrical aspects of a situation or object of study. Thus, one can explore the 'performative' aspects of, say, a church service, parliament, or a public lecture.

Perlocution, perlocutionary effect The perlocutionary aspect of an utterance is any effect it achieves on its hearers or readers that is a consequence of what is said. When the police officer orders me to get out of the car and place my hands on my head, the order may precipitate any number of responses from me, such as anger, fear, resignation, obedience, or an attempt to escape. Such responses are the perlocutionary effects of the order; they are not produced by the conformity of a particular utterance to a set of felicity conditions, so they are not predictable or regular.

Pragmatics The pragmatic analysis of language studies how language works in the world as a practice or practical instrument; it thus attends not to meaning understood as the concept or idea signified by a particular word or words but to meaning as it emerges from the interactions of language users.

Queer theory   A form of critical and political interrogation of concepts and constructions of identity, informed by both feminist thinking on sex, gender and desire and the demands of gay political activism. Queer theory is not just a theory of sexuality or homosexuality; rather, it seeks to show how the categorising work undertaken by such ideas can and should be undone. So queer theory and criticism does not assume that there are specific sexual identities that are then the object of cultural or linguistic representation. Instead, a queer theoretical approach will seek to show how such identities are both the product of representational strategies and can be exposed to challenge.

Speech act   The linguistic unit sufficient to bring about a particular illocutionary action in the right circumstances or 'speech situation'. Austin coined the term to describe the active character of our utterances, what we *do* in speaking. A speech act can be written as well as oral: a written will is as much a speech act as a verbal command.

Transcendental   In his later work the eighteenth century German philosopher Immanuel Kant sought to outline the necessary conditions of experience, the conditions that must be in place for experience to be possible. Such conditions are therefore transcendental in their relation to our actual, worldly experience: they are not elements within it, but its formal preconditions. For Kant, the unity of the conscious subject of experience could be described in these terms as transcendental. Subsequent thinkers have suggested that other elements, such as language, might also be transcendental.

FURTHER READING

Austin, J. (1975) *How to Do Things With Words*, J. O. Urmson and Marina Sbisa (eds), 2nd edition, Oxford: Clarendon Press.
> The series of twelve lectures given by Austin at Harvard University in 1955, edited for publication only after his death. It is a crucial text that all those seeking to make sense of theories of performativity will need to explore. Written for oral delivery in an accessible if not breezy style, it nonetheless requires careful reading if common misunderstandings are to be avoided.

Austin, J. (1979) *Philosophical Papers*, J. O. Urmson and G. J. Warnock (eds), 3rd edition, Oxford: Oxford University Press.
> A collection of Austin's essays, this book provides invaluable context for the Harvard lectures. Of particular relevance are 'Other Minds', 'A Plea for Excuses', 'Pretending' and 'Three Ways of Spilling Ink'.

Bennington, G., and Derrida J. (1993) *Jacques Derrida*, Chicago: The University of Chicago Press.
> The bulk of this book is taken up with Geoffrey Bennington's lucid exposition of Derrida's thinking, organised around prominent motifs or themes. A valuable introduction to his work.

Butler, J. (1997) *Excitable Speech: A Politics of the Performative*, New York and London: Routledge.
> Butler's most extensive elaboration of her theory of performativity *per se*, in the context of philosophical, political and legal debates around the performative power of language.

Butler, J. (1999) *Gender Trouble: Feminism and the Subversion of Identity*, 2nd edition, New York and London: Routledge.
> The now classic exposition of Butler's thinking on the ways in which categories of identity might be understood in the terms offered by a theory of performativity.

Cavell, S. (1979) *The Claim of Reason: Wittgenstein, Skepticism, Morality, and Tragedy*, Oxford: University of Oxford Press.
> Cavell's most influential exposition of his approach to philosophy, clearly demonstrating his differing debts to Austin and to Wittgenstein, and dwelling on the political and ethical implications of his stance.

Cavell, S. (1994) *A Pitch of Philosophy: Autobiographical Exercises*, Cambridge, Massachusetts: Harvard University Press.
The core of this book is an extensive meditation on Austin's Harvard lectures, in critical dialogue with Derrida's influential engagement with the same text. Usefully addresses some of the ways in which the standard understanding of Austin in literary critical circles might require adjustment.

Cavell, S. (2002) *Must We Mean What We Say?*, updated edition, Cambridge: Cambridge University Press.
The title essay of this collection is a clear and forcefully argued defence of Austin against the criticisms of philosophers from the logical positivist tradition. A fuller sense of Cavell's developing thought can be gained from the essays entitled 'Austin at Criticism', 'The Availability of Wittgenstein's Later Philosophy', and 'Aesthetic Problems of Modern Philosophy' in particular.

de Man, P. (1979) *Allegories of Reading: Figural Language in Rousseau, Nietzsche, Rilke, and Proust*, New Haven: Yale University Press.
Paul de Man's distinctive, sometimes difficult formulation of the deconstructive approach to reading is given its most extensive elaboration in this series of linked essays. The terms of speech act theory are appropriated and appear here in new light; of particular relevance are the concluding essays on the promise and the excuse.

Derrida, J. (1988) *Limited Inc*, trans. S. Weber, Evanston: Chicago University Press.
Gathered together here are Derrida's original essay on Austin, 'Signature Event Context', 'Limited Inc a b c . . . ', his polemical response to Searle, and the helpful clarification of an 'Afterword' in which Derrida deals with questions put to him by readers of the earlier works. This is inevitably a challenging read, but an essential reference point for all subsequent discussions.

Derrida, J. (2002) *Without Alibi*, trans. P. Kamuf, Stanford: Stanford University Press.
Contains the important late essay 'Typewriter Ribbon: Limited Ink (2)' in which Derrida returns to Austin via a meditation on Paul de Man's *Allegories of Reading*.

Eldridge, R. (ed.) (2003) *Stanley Cavell*, Cambridge: Cambridge University Press
A collection of essays by a range of different readers of Cavell's work, picking up both on his debt to and development of Austin, and on the implications of his approach to and through the 'ordinary'. Most suitable for those already familiar with some aspects of Cavell.

Felman, S. (2002) *The Scandal of the Speaking Body: Don Juan with J. L. Austin, or Seduction in Two Languages*, trans. C. Porter, Stanford: Stanford University Press.

Originally published in French in 1980, this is an excitingly strong reading of
Austin with Don Juan and the psychoanalytic thinking of Jacques Lacan. An
important text in its own right, but also a formative influence for Judith
Butler. In this edition, it is bookended by helpful essays from Cavell and
Butler.

Gasché, R. (1986) *The Tain of the Mirror: Derrida and the Philosophy of Reflection*,
Cambridge, Massachusetts: Harvard University Press.
A densely argued, classic if not unchallenged reading of Derrida's work. Not
for the beginner, necessarily, but does contain an influential account of how
'iterability' finds its place within the movement of Derrida's thought.

Hammer, E. (2002) *Stanley Cavell: Skepticism, Subjectivity and the Ordinary*,
Cambridge: Polity Press.
A clearly argued and concise introduction to the range of Cavell's work, this
is a very useful book for those new to his approach to philosophy.

Petrey, S. (1990) *Speech Acts and Literary Theory*, New York and London: Routledge.
A helpful account of the development of Austin's ideas on the performative
in the particular context of literary theory and criticism. Petrey provides a
strong 'conventionalist' reading of Austin which is a useful counterpoint to
Searle's 'intentionalist' model.

Schechner, R. (2002) *Performance Studies: An Introduction*, New York and London:
Routledge.
Schechner's comprehensive, introductory overview of the discipline of per-
formance studies, within which performance theory takes a prominent place.
The way in which the Austinian heritage is incorporated into performance
theory is here given a clear exposition.

Searle, J. (1969) *Speech Acts: An Essay in the Philosophy of Language*, Cambridge:
Cambridge University Press.
A methodical and highly influential exposition of 'speech act theory', devel-
oping both out of and away from Austin's account.

Searle, J. (1979) *Expression and Meaning: Studies in the Theory of Speech Acts*,
Cambridge: Cambridge University Press.
This collection of essays contains Searle's essay on 'The Logical Status of
Fictional Discourse', and is an important effort to tidy a range of linguistic
peculiarities into the framework elaborated in *Speech Acts*.

Sedgwick, E. (2003) *Touching Feeling: Affect, Pedagogy, Performativity*, Durham:
Duke University Press.
Contains two essays and an introduction in which Sedgwick's distinctive
approach to the performative is set out, and which make clear both her

affinities with, and differences from, the more systematically argued approach of Butler.

Sedgwick, E. and Parker, A. (eds) (1995) *Performativity and Performance*, New York and London: Routledge.
A collection of essays which in various ways explore the relation between the thinking of performativity since Austin and the theory and practice of performance.

REFERENCES

Adorno, T. W. and Horkheimer, M (1972) *Dialectic of Enlightenment*, trans. J. Cumming, New York: Herder and Herder.

Affeldt, S (1998) 'The Ground of Mutuality: Criteria, Judgment and Intelligibility in Stephen Mulhall and Stanley Cavell', *European Journal of Philosophy* 6: 1–31.

Althusser, L (1971) 'Ideology and Ideological State Apparatuses', in *Lenin and Philosophy and other Essays*, trans. B. Brewster, London: New Left Books.

Apel, K-O. (1991) 'Is Intentionality more Basic than Linguistic Meaning?', in E. Lapore and R. van Gullick (eds) *John Searle and His Critics*, Oxford: Blackwell, 31–55.

—— (1998) *From a Transcendental-Semiotic Point of View*, M. Papastephanou (ed.), Manchester: Manchester University Press.

Artaud, A. (1970) *The Theatre and Its Double*, trans. V. Corti, London: John Calder.

—— (1988) *Selected Writings*, S. Sontag (ed.), Berkeley: University of California Press.

Auslander, P. (1999) *Liveness: Performance in a Mediatized Culture*, New York and London: Routledge.

Austin, J. L. (1962) *Sense and Sensibilia*, G. J. Warnock (ed.), Oxford: Oxford University Press.

—— (1963) 'Performative-Constative', trans. G. J. Warnock, in C. E. Caton (ed.), *Philosophy and Ordinary Language*, Urbana: University of Illinois Press, 22–54.

—— (1975) *How to Do Things With Words*, J. O. Urmson and Marina Sbisa (eds), 2nd edition, Oxford: Clarendon Press.

—— (1979) *Philosophical Papers*, J. O. Urmson and G. J. Warnock (eds), 3rd edition, Oxford: Oxford University Press.

Ayer, A. J. (1936) *Language, Truth and Logic*, London: Gollancz.

Bearn, G. (1995) 'Derrida Dry: Iterating Iterability Analytically', *Diacritics*, 25.3: 2–25.

Bell, V. (1999) 'On Speech, Race, and Melancholia: an Interview with Judith Butler', *Theory, Culture and Society*, 16: 163–74.

Bernstein, J. (2003) 'Aesthetics, Modernism, Literature: Cavell's Transformations of Philosophy', in Richard Eldridge (ed.), *Stanley Cavell*, Cambridge: Cambridge University Press, 107–42.

Bourdieu, P. (1991) *Language and Symbolic Power*, trans. G. Raymond and M. Adamson, J. Thompson (ed.), Cambridge: Polity.

Brecht, B. (1964) *Brecht on Theatre: the Development of an Aesthetic*, trans. J. Willett, London: Methuen.

Brodsky Lacour, C. (1992) 'The Temporality of Convention: Convention Theory and Romanticism', in M. Hjort (ed.), *Rules and Conventions: Literature, Philosophy, Social Theory*, Baltimore: Johns Hopkins University Press, 274–93.

Butler, J. (1990) 'Performative Acts and Gender Constitution: An Essay in Phenomenology and Feminist Theory', in S. Case (ed.), *Performing Feminisms: Feminist Critical Theory and Theatre*, Baltimore: Johns Hopkins University Press, 270–82.

—— (1993) *Bodies That Matter: On the Discursive Limits of Sex*, New York and London: Routledge.

—— (1997a) *Excitable Speech: A Politics of the Performative*, New York and London: Routledge.

—— (1997b) *The Psychic Life of Power: Theories in Subjection*, Stanford: Stanford University Press.

—— (1999) *Gender Trouble: Feminism and the Subversion of Identity*, 2nd edition, New York and London: Routledge.

—— (2000) *Antigone's Claim: Kinship Between Life and Death*, New York: Columbia University Press.

—— (2002) 'Afterword', in S. Felman, *The Scandal of the Speaking Body: Don Juan with J. L. Austin, or Seduction in Two Languages*, trans. C. Porter, Stanford: Stanford University Press, 113–23.

—— (2004) *Undoing Gender*, New York and London: Routledge.

—— (2005) *Giving an Account of Oneself*, New York: Fordham.

Cavell, S. (1979) *The Claim of Reason: Wittgenstein, Skepticism, Morality, and Tragedy*, Oxford: University of Oxford Press.

—— (1984) *Themes Out of School: Effects and Causes*, San Francisco: North Point Press.

—— (1994) *A Pitch of Philosophy: Autobiographical Exercises*, Cambridge, Massachusetts: Harvard University Press.

—— (2002) *Must We Mean What We Say?*, updated edition, Cambridge: Cambridge University Press.

—— (2005) *Philosophy the Day After Tomorrow*, Cambridge, Massachusetts: Belknap Press.

Chase, C. (1986) *Decomposing Figures: Rhetorical Readings in the Romantic Tradition*, Baltimore: Johns Hopkins University Press.

Conquergood, D. (2002) 'Performance Studies: Interventions and Radical Research', *The Drama Review*, 46: 145–56.

Culler, J. (1983) *On Deconstruction: Theory and Criticism After Structuralism*, London: Routledge and Kegan Paul.

Dasenbrock, R. (ed.) (1989) *Redrawing the Lines: Analytic Philosophy, Deconstruction, and Literary Theory*, Minneapolis: University of Minnesota Press.

de Man, P. (1979) *Allegories of Reading: Figural Language in Rousseau, Nietzsche, Rilke, and Proust*, New Haven: Yale University Press.

—— (1986) *The Resistance to Theory*, Minneapolis: University of Minnesota Press.

Derrida, J. (1978) *Writing and Difference*, trans. A. Bass, London: Routledge and Kegan Paul.

—— (1988) *Limited Inc*, trans. S. Weber, Evanston: Chicago University Press.

—— (1989a) *Memoires: for Paul de Man*, trans. C. Lindsay, J. Culler, E. Cadava and P. Kamuf, revised edition, New York: Columbia University Press.

—— (1989b) 'Psyche: Inventions of the Other', trans. C. Porter, in L. Waters and W. Godzich (eds), *Reading de Man Reading*, Minneapolis: University of Minnesota Press, 25–65.

—— (1992a) 'Before the Law', in D. Attridge (ed.), *Acts of Literature*, New York and London, 181–220.

—— (1992b) 'Force of Law: The "Mystical Foundation of Authority"', trans. M. Quaintance, in D. Cornell, M. Rosenfeld and D. Gray Carson (eds), *Deconstruction and the Possibility of Justice*, New York and London: Routledge, 3–67.

—— (1994) *Specters of Marx*, trans. P. Kamuf, New York and London: Routledge.

—— (1997) *The Politics of Friendship*, trans. G. Collins, London: Verso.

—— (2000) 'Performative Powerlessness – A Response to Simon Critchley', trans. J. Ingram, *Constellations*, 7: 466–68.

—— (2002a) *Without Alibi*, trans. P. Kamuf, Stanford: Stanford University Press.

—— (2002b) *Negotiations*, trans. E. Rottenberg, Stanford: Stanford University Press.

—— (2005) *Rogues: Two Essays on Reason*, trans. P-A. Brault and M. Naas, Stanford: Stanford University Press.

Derrida, J. and Dufourmantelle, A., (2000) *Of Hospitality*, trans. R. Bowlby, Stanford: Stanford University Press.

Felman, S. (2002) *The Scandal of the Speaking Body: Don Juan with J. L. Austin, or Seduction in Two Languages*, trans. C. Porter, Stanford: Stanford University Press.

Fish, S. (1980) *Is There a Text in This Class? The Authority of Interpretive Communities*, Cambridge, Massachusetts: Harvard University Press.

Fotion, N. (2000) *John Searle*, Teddington: Acumen.

Foucault, M. (1977) *Discipline and Punish: the Birth of the Prison*, trans. A. Sheridan, London: Allen Lane.

—— (1979) *The History of Sexuality, Vol. 1: An Introduction*, trans. R. Hurley, London: Allen Lane.

—— (1980) *Power/Knowledge*, trans. C. Gordon, Brighton: Harvester Press.

Fusco, C. (1994) 'The Other History of Intercultural Performance', *The Drama Review*, 38: 143–67.

Goffman, E. (1959) *The Presentation of Self in Everyday Life*, New York: Doubleday.

Gorman, D. (1999) 'The Use and Abuse of Speech-Act Theory in Criticism', *Poetics Today*, 20: 93–119.

Habermas, J. (1984) *The Theory of Communicative Action, Vol. 1: Reason and the Rationalization of Society*, trans. T. McCarthy, London: Heinemann.

—— (1987) *The Theory of Communicative Action, Vol. 2: Lifeworld and System*, trans. T. McCarthy, Cambridge: Polity Press.

—— (1999) *On the Pragmatics of Communication*, M. Cooke (ed.), Cambridge: Polity Press.

Hamacher, W., Hertz, N. and Keenan, T. (eds) (1989) *Responses: On Paul de Man's Wartime Journalism*, Lincoln: University of Nebraska Press.

Harris, G. (1999) *Staging Femininities: Performance and Performativity*, Manchester: Manchester University Press.

Hill, G. (1984) 'Our Word is Our Bond', in *The Lords of Limit: Essays on Literature and Ideas*, London: Andre Deutsch, 138–60.

Huizinga, J. (1950) *Homo Ludens: A Study of the Play Element in Culture*, New York: Beacon Press.

Jackson, S. (2004) *Professing Performance: Theatre in the Academy from Philology to Performativity*, Cambridge: Cambridge University Press.

Kaprow, A. (1993) *Essays on the Blurring of Art and Life*, Berkeley: University of California Press.

Kirby, M. (ed.) (1965) *Happenings: An Illustrated Anthology*, New York: Dutton.

Lewis, D. (1969) *Convention: A Philosophical Study*, Cambridge, Massachusetts: Harvard University Press.

Mackinnon, C. (1993) *Only Words*, Cambridge, Massachusetts: Harvard University Press.

Mates, B. (1964) 'On the Verification of Statements about Ordinary Language', in V. C. Chappell (ed.), *Ordinary Language: Essays in Philosophical Method*, Englewood Cliffs: Prentice-Hall, 64–74.

McKenzie, J. (2001) *Perform or Else: From Discipline to Performance*, New York and London: Routledge.

Miller, J. H. (2001) *Speech Acts in Literature*, Stanford: Stanford University Press.

Mulhall, S. (2003) 'Stanley Cavell's Vision of the Normativity of Language: Grammar, Criteria, and Rules', in Richard Eldridge (ed.), *Stanley Cavell*, Cambridge: Cambridge University Press, 79–106.

Murdoch, I. (1965) *The Red and the Green*, London: Chatto and Windus.

Nerlich, B. and Clarke, D (1996) *Language, Action and Context: The Early History of Pragmatics in Europe and America*, Amsterdam: J. Benjamins.

Newton, E. (1972) *Mother Camp: Female Impersonators in America*, Englewood Cliffs: Prentice-Hall.

Petrey, S. (1990) *Speech Acts and Literary Theory*, New York and London: Routledge.

Phelan, P. (1993) *Unmarked: The Politics of Performance*, New York and London: Routledge.

Quine, W. (1969) 'Foreword', in D. Lewis, *Convention: A Philosophical Study*, Cambridge, Massachusetts: Harvard University Press, xi-xii.

Reinelt, J. (2002) 'The Politics of Discourse: Performativity Meets Theatricality', *SubStance*, 31: 201–15.

Ricks, C. (1996) 'Austin's Swink', in *Essays in Appreciation*, Oxford: Clarendon Press, 260–79.

Schechner, R. (1985) *Between Theater and Anthropology*, Philadelphia: University of Pennsylvania Press.

—— (1988) *Performance Theory*, revised edition, New York and London: Routledge.

—— (1993) *The Future of Ritual: Writings on Culture and Performance*, New York and London: Routledge.

—— (2002) *Performance Studies: An Introduction*, New York and London: Routledge.

Schneider, R. (1997) *The Explicit Body in Performance*, New York and London: Routledge.

Searle, J. (1969) *Speech Acts: An Essay in the Philosophy of Language*, Cambridge: Cambridge University Press.

—— (1977) 'Reiterating the Differences: A Reply to Derrida', *Glyph* 1: 198–208.

—— (1979) *Expression and Meaning: Studies in the Theory of Speech Acts*, Cambridge: Cambridge University Press.

—— (1983) 'The Word Turned Upside Down', *New York Review of Books*, 30: 16: 74–79.

—— (1989) 'How Performatives Work', *Linguistics and Philosophy*, 12: 535–58.

—— (1994) 'Literary Theory and Its Discontents', *New Literary History*, 25: 637–67.

—— (2001) *Rationality in Action*, Cambridge, Massachusetts: MIT Press.

Searle, J. and Vanderveken, D. (1985) *Foundations of Illocutionary Logic*, Cambridge: Cambridge University Press.

Sedgwick, E. (2003) *Touching Feeling: Affect, Pedagogy, Performativity*, Durham: Duke University Press.

Sidney, P. ([1595] 1966) *A Defence of Poetry*, J. Van Dorsten (ed.), Oxford: Oxford University Press.

Skinner, Q. (1988) 'A Reply to my Critics', in J. Tully (ed.), *Meaning and Context: Quentin Skinner and his Critics*, Princeton: Princeton University Press, 231–88.

Smith, B. (1990) 'Towards a History of Speech Act Theory', in A. Burckhardt (ed.), *Speech Acts, Meanings and Intentions: Critical Approaches to the Philosophy of John Searle*, Berlin and New York: de Gruyer.

Sprinkle, A. (1998) *Post Porn Modernist: My 25 Years as a Multi-media Whore*, San Francisco: Cleis Press.

Tambiah, S. (1985) *Culture, Thought and Social Action: An Anthropological Perspective*, Cambridge, Massachusetts: Harvard University Press.

Taylor, D. (1998) 'A Savage Performance: Guillermo Gómez-Peña and Coco Fusco's "Couple in the Cage"', *The Drama Review*, 42: 160–75.

Turner, V. (1969) *The Ritual Process: Structure and Anti-Structure*, London: Routledge and Kegan Paul.

—— (1974) *Dramas, Fields and Metaphors: Symbolic Action in Human Society*, Ithaca: Cornell University Press.

—— (1982) *From Ritual to Theatre: The Human Seriousness of Play*, New York: PAJ Publications.

—— (1987) *The Anthropology of Performance*, New York: PAJ Publications.

Wittgenstein, L. (2001) *Philosophical Investigations*, trans. G. Anscombe, 3rd edition, Oxford: Blackwell.

INDEX

ROUTLEDGE CRITICAL THINKERS

Series Editor: Robert Eaglestone,
Royal Holloway, University of London

Routledge Critical Thinkers is designed for students who need an accessible introduction to the key figures in contemporary critical thought. The books provide crucial orientation for further study and equip readers to engage with each theorist's original texts.

'These little books are certainly helpful study guides. They are clear, concise and complete. They are ideal for undergraduates studying for exams or writing essays and for lifelong learners wanting to expand their knowledge of a given author or idea.'
Beth Lord, *THES*

'This series demystifies the demigods of theory.'
Susan Bennett, *University of Calgary*

Available at all good bookshops
For further information on individual books in the series, visit:
www.routledge.com/literature/rct

RELATED TITLES FROM ROUTLEDGE

JEAN BAUDRILLARD
Richard J. Lane

Routledge *Critical* Thinkers series

'An uncommonly successful introduction to Jean Baudrillard.'
Charles Acland, *Concordia University, Canada*

Jean Baudrillard is one of the most famous and controversial of writers on postmodernism. But what are his key ideas? Where did they come from and why are they important? This book offers a beginner's guide to Baudrillard's thought, including his views on:

- technology
- primitivism
- reworking Marxism
- simulation and the hyperreal
- America and postmodernism

Richard J. Lane places Baudrillard's ideas in the context of French and postmodern thought and examines the ongoing impact of his work. This is the perfect companion for any student approaching the work of Jean Baudrillard.

ISBN10: 0-415-21514-5 (hbk)
ISBN10: 0-415-21515-3 (pbk)

ISBN13: 978-0-415-21514-5 (hbk)
ISBN13: 978-0-415-21515-2 (pbk)

Available at all good bookshops
For further information on our literature series, please visit
www.routledge.com/literature/series.asp
For ordering and further information please visit:
www.routledge.com

RELATED TITLES FROM ROUTLEDGE

JACQUES DERRIDA

Nicholas Royle

Routledge *Critical* Thinkers series

'Excellent, strong, clear and original'
Jacques Derrida – commenting on this volume

'A strong, inventive and daring book that does much more than most
introductions are capable of dreaming'
Diane Elam, *Cardiff University*

'Readers couldn't ask for a more authoritative and knowledgeable guide.
Although there is no playing down of the immensity of Derrida's work,
Royle's direct and often funny mode of address will make it less threat-
ening than it can often appear to beginners.'
Derek Attridge

There are few figures more important in literary and critical theory than
Jacques Derrida. Whether lauded or condemned, his writing has had
far-reaching ramifications, and his work on deconstruction cannot be
ignored. Nicholas Royle's unique book, written in an innovative and
original style, is an outstanding introduction to the methods and significance of Jacques Derrida.

ISBN10: 0-415-22930-8 (hbk)
ISBN10: 0-415-22931-6 (pbk)

ISBN13: 978-0-415-22930-2 (hbk)
ISBN13: 978-0-415-22931-9 (pbk)

Available at all good bookshops
For further information on our literature series, please visit
www.routledge.com/literature/series.asp
For ordering and further information please visit:
www.routledge.com

RELATED TITLES FROM ROUTLEDGE

PERFORMANCE:
A Critical Introduction 2nd Edition
Marvin Carlson

Performance: A Critical Introduction was the first textbook to provide an overview of the modern concept of performance and its development in various related fields. This comprehensively revised, illustrated edition discusses recent performance work and takes into consideration changes that have taken place since the book's original publication in 1996. Marvin Carlson guides the reader through the contested definition of performance as a theatrical activity and the myriad ways in which performance has been interpreted by ethnographers, anthropologists, linguists, and cultural theorists.

Topics covered include:

- the evolution of performance art since the 1960s
- the relationship between performance, postmodernism, the politics of identity, and current cultural studies
- the recent theoretical developments in the study of performance in the fields of anthropology, psychoanalysis, linguistics, and technology.

With a fully updated bibliography and additional glossary of terms, students of performance studies, visual and performing arts or theatre history will welcome this new version of a classic text.

ISBN10: 0-415-29926-8 (hbk)
ISBN10: 0-415-29927-6 (pbk)

ISBN13: 978-0-415-29926-8 (hbk)
ISBN13: 978-0-415-29927-5 (pbk)

Available at all good bookshops
For ordering and further information please visit:
www.routledge.com

RELATED TITLES FROM ROUTLEDGE

PERFORMANCE THEORY

Richard Schechner

'*Performance Theory* is Richard Schechner's classic contribution to the performing arts and critical theory.'
Homi K. Bhabha, *Harvard University*

Few have had quite as much impact in both the academy and in the world of theatre production as Richard Schechner. His view that drama is not just something that occurs on stage, but something that happens in everyday life, full of meaning, and on many different levels, challenged conventional definitions of theatre, ritual and performance. This Routledge Classics edition includes a new preface in which the author looks back at the field he was so instrumental in creating. Schechner redefined what performance means, and in doing so, has contested the boundaries that separated audience and actor ever since.

ISBN10: 0–415–31455–0 9 (pbk)
ISBN13: 978-0-415-31455-8 (pbk)

Available at all good bookshops
For ordering and further information please visit:
www.routledge.com